COLLECTING
GLASS
The Facts At Your Fingertips

COLLECTING
GLASS
The Facts At Your Fingertips

Sarah Yates

Special Consultants:
Mark West
David McCarron

Collecting Glass
The Facts At Your Fingertips

First published in Great Britain in 2000 by Miller's, an imprint of
Mitchell Beazley, both divisions of Octopus Publishing Group Ltd,
2–4 Heron Quays,
Docklands, London E14 4JP

© 2000 Octopus Publishing Group Ltd

Miller's is a registered trademark of Octopus Publishing Group Ltd

Commissioning Editor Anna Sanderson
Executive Art Editor Vivienne Brar
Senior Art Editors Rhonda Fisher, Lucy Parissi
Project Editor Emily Anderson
Editors Anne Crane, Claire Musters
Proofreader Laura Hicks
Designer Louise Griffiths
Picture Research Maria Gibbs
Production Catherine Lay
Indexer Hilary Bird
Contributors Jill Bace and Frankie Leibe

A CIP catalogue record for this book is available from
the British Library

ISBN 1 84000 191 7

Set in Bembo
Produced by Toppan Printing Co., (HK) Ltd.
Printed and bound in China

Front cover *(Clockwise from top left)* Heart-shaped vase by
Flavio Poli, *c.*1956, £500–800/$800–1,275; Lynn glass
decanter, *c.*1790, £1,500–2,500/$2,400–4,000; Salviati
cup and saucer, *c.*1920, £120–150/$200–240; *Historismus*
beaker, *c.*1880, £120–180/$190–290; scent bottles with
box, *c.*1850, £500–700/$800–1,125; *façon de Venise* glass,
16thC, £20,000–25,000/$32,000–40,000
Front flap Sulphide plaque of King George IV by
Apsley Pellatt, *c.*1820, £3,000–4,000/$4,800–6,400.
Back cover Covered tankard by Johann Joseph Mildner,
*c.*1787, £14,000–17,000/$22,400–27,000.
Back flap *(left)* Enamelled glass by Fritz Heckert, *c.*1900,
£140–200/$225–320; *(right)* engraved *Roemer* by
J. & L. Lobmeyr, *c.*1890, £150–200/$240–320.
Page 2 *(Clockwise from top left)* Opalescent "Vaseline" glass
vase, 1870s, £300–500/$475–800; American amberina

"slug" jug by Joseph Locke, *c.*1880, £400–600/$650–950;
Baccarat hock glass, *c.*1890, £200–250/$325–400; Gothic
Revival decanter by W.H., B. & J. Richardson, *c.*1835,
£350–500/$560–800; "Maine" pattern goblet, *c.*1899,
£125–250/$200–400; blue and white swirl carafe by St
Louis, *c.*1850, £600–650/$950–1,040; leaf pattern vase by
W. Clyne Farquharson, 1936, £700–900/$1,125–1,440;
enamelled Theresienthaler hock glass, *c.*1900, £120–150/
$200–240; Arts & Crafts decanter, *c.*1890, £200–300/
$325–475; Irish boat-shaped bowl, £2,000–3,000/$3,200–4,800.
Page 3 *(Clockwise from top left)* Cut-glass bowl, *c.*1928,
£700–900/$1,125–1,440; green "Depression" glass jug,
1930s, £40–55/$65–90; Japanese-style vase, late 19thC,
£350–500/$560–800; pink dish, *c.*1920,
£400–480/$650–775; amethyst ship's decanter, *c.*1800,
£650–750/$1,050–1,200

CONTENTS

INTRODUCTION

Glass is probably one of the most undervalued, yet versatile and intriguing, materials used in the applied arts: it is a super-cooled liquid, yet it feels warm to the touch; one of its main components is sand, yet it can be crystal clear or made in all the colours of the rainbow; it is hard, yet breaks into a thousand pieces; and, although often light, glass vessels can hold many times their own weight. From ancient times glass has been used for making not only expensive luxury objects but also practical tableware and vessels. One of the greatest advantages for collectors today is that much antique glass is less expensive than ceramics or silver of a similar date, while some late Georgian and Victorian table glass can cost not much more than good-quality modern glassware.

Watch someone with an attractive glass full of any drink, be it lemonade, wine or water, and you will start to see the spell glass can cast. If you have a beautiful painting you can merely admire it, but a drinking glass is designed to be held in the hand, and often employed as a prop during conversation. One would never think to hold a plate of food to the light to admire the colour, but it is almost automatic with a glass of wine; one does not knock on a dining-table to hear the sound, but tapping or "pinging" a glass with the fingers to hear it ring is quite normal. Elegant drinking glasses and decanters can often enhance the enjoyment of good food and wine – and even a mediocre wine often seems to taste better when poured into a beautiful cut or engraved glass. Despite its fragility, much antique glassware can be surprisingly robust, and requires little specialist attention – used for special occasions and dinner parties, it can simply be washed and stored away again. A friend of mine was invited to rather a smart dinner party where drinks were presented in some tall modern glasses. As the meal wound down, and the conversation became more animated, my friend was emphasizing a point to his neighbour and the stem of the glass came away in his hand; covered in confusion he turned to his none-too-impressed hostess,

picked up the glass next to him, and explained how the accident had happened, whereupon the second glass disintegrated. Of course, I am sure this would never happen with antique drinking glasses!

Many people acquire glassware through inheritance or as wedding presents; only in a few cases do they start from scratch when buying glass to use. By all means keep "best" glasses for special occasions and have more robust, durable pieces for everyday use, but, as with a collection proper, do spend time finding what you really like before you begin buying them.

Whether you buy glass to use or to admire, always take advantage of dealers' wealth of practical knowledge, and visit museums to increase your visual awareness. Also read about and research your chosen area of collecting, as even an expensive reference book will have paid for itself if it saves you a costly blunder. Bear in mind that uses and types of glass have changed many times over the years: a case in point is the brandy balloon drinking glass. Ever since a brandy producer featured a Napoleonic officer with such a glass in its advertisements many people seem to think, mistakenly, that this type of glass dates from the early 19thC. Some years ago I did a little research into this and could find no evidence of brandy balloons on manufacturers' lists before the late 1940s; it is possible they were produced in limited numbers in the early 20thC, but most certainly never in Napoleon's time.

One of the other main reasons for buying old glass is profit. I think that those who come to dealing from collecting take a difficult route, as they will always be tempted to keep the best of what they buy and therefore tend to sell their own rejects. To become a professional dealer involves either many early mornings, long drives and hours trying to sell to sceptical customers, or considerable amounts of money to acquire stock to compete with the established trade. I know people who have become very successful via one route or the other, although many more are less fortunate and are left poorer and wiser, but also, perhaps, with some happy memories and a few nice pieces of glass.

Whatever the reasons for buying antique glass, be it use, collecting or profit, it is very important to handle glassware. Styles in glass tend to repeat themselves, and purely visual knowledge can often be insufficient in telling the difference between a copy and an original. Auction previews can be a good place to examine items, particularly as some pieces at auction are so rare and valuable that you would only otherwise see them in a museum.

Like most forms of collecting, buying glass can become a bug. Always remember the golden rules of collecting: buy the least number of items for the most money as top-quality pieces will always be saleable if you find that you want or need to part with your collection. Similarly, only buy what you like and feel that you can live with. I hope that through this book you will enjoy building up a glass collection, and come to understand the magic and see the beauty of antique glass.

MARK WEST

The values given in this book for featured objects reflect the sort of prices you might expect to pay for similar pieces at an auction house or from a dealer. As there are so many variable factors involved in the pricing of antiques, such as the condition of the item, where you purchase it and market trends, the values given should be used as a general guide only.

PERIODS & STYLES

CLASSICAL

- **Period** from c.1500 BC (ancient Egypt); from 1st century BC (ancient Roman Empire)
- **Areas of origin** Egypt; Roman Empire (present-day Syria, Jordan and Israel)
- **Characteristics** heavy forms, often bright blue (Egypt); uneven decoration; pale blue/green, lightweight, iridescent (Roman Empire)
- **Forms** inlay (Egypt); small oil flasks and bottles, funerary jars; vases; figurines
- **Decoration** combing; trailing mosaic glass

BAROQUE

- **Period** late 17thC to early 18thC
- **Areas of origin** Central Europe and Bohemia; Low Countries
- **Characteristics** heavy, thick-walled glass; improved quality potash glass
- **Forms** presentation pieces; lidded goblets; beakers; drinking glasses
- **Decoration** ornate wheel engraving and enamelling; diamond-point engraving; stipple engraving; hunting scenes; coats of arms

GEORGIAN

- **Period** c.1730–1800
- **Areas of origin** England; France; Low Countries
- **Characteristics** lead glass with grey tone; emphasis on form; restrained style
- **Forms** small-bowled drinking glasses and goblets; decanters
- **Decoration** wheel-engraving; enamelling; gilding (flowers and vine leaves); political and commemorative; colour and air-twist stems

REGENCY

- **Period** c.1805–1830s
- **Areas of origin** England; Ireland; copied elsewhere in continental Europe
- **Characteristics** square solid shapes with straight lines; heavy, balanced, practical forms
- **Forms** sturdy short-stemmed rummers; large-bodied, short-necked decanters and jugs; boat-shaped bowls; butter dishes
- **Decoration** elaborate all-over cutting; some decanters, glasses, bottles in one solid colour

VICTORIAN

- **Period** 1830s–*c*.1900
- **Areas of origin** worldwide, but particularly Europe and the USA
- **Characteristics** technological innovation for international exhibitions; mass-produced glass; heavy architectural shapes; simpler styles in 1870s with Arts and Crafts Movement
- **Forms** sets of tableware; vases; lighting; jugs
- **Decoration** elaborate; colouring; flashing; acid-etching; engraving; cameo; casing and staining

ART NOUVEAU

- **Period** 1880s to World War I
- **Areas of origin** France; USA; Belgium; Austria; Britain
- **Characteristics** art glass (handmade pieces by individuals); rejection of factory production
- **Forms** decorative pieces; vases; bowls; lamps; curving sinuous lines based on natural plant and flower forms
- **Decoration** integral; iridescence; frosted finishes; cameo; engraved lilies, irises, pansies

ART DECO

- **Period** 1920s–1930s
- **Areas of origin** France; USA; Bohemia
- **Characteristics** bold colour, shape and pattern; collectable pieces by individual artists such as René Lalique (1860–1945)
- **Forms** heavy, thick, geometric shapes; vases; figural sculpture; lamps; perfume bottles; decanters; drinking glasses
- **Decoration** cutting; enamelling; press-moulding; acid-etching

POST-WAR

- **Period** post 1945
- **Areas of origin** Scandinavia; Italy; USA
- **Characteristics** emphasis on artist's name; unique designer pieces, made to commission
- **Forms** decorative pieces; vases; bowls; sculptural and organic shapes; often free-blown; domesticware
- **Decoration** extremely diverse, often integral to the form; experimentation with bold colour and texture; lampwork

PART 1

BUYING & SELLING
GLASS

ABOVE AN ENGRAVED CRANBERRY GLASS JUG,
c.1870, £150–250/$240–400.

LEFT A SELECTION OF CLEAR GLASS DECANTERS

STARTING A COLLECTION

Glass is, surprisingly, one of the most affordable types of antique available to the novice collector today. Many pieces are less expensive than small silver or porcelain items, while good-quality antique glassware may cost less than a similar modern piece. Another point to bear in mind when beginning your collection is that though old glass may not increase dramatically in value it will at least hold its price, unlike modern glass which depreciates in value immediately after purchase. For this reason many glass enthusiasts prefer to buy antique glass to use, especially sets of glass tableware such as drinking glasses and decanters. Throughout history, glass has been made in an infinite range of styles, forms and colours, so you are certain to find something that you like.

Whether you buy to use, for investment, or for aesthetic pleasure only, spend some time finding out what type of glass appeals to you, and what you can afford. Consider how you will display your collection and how much time you will spend building up and caring for it. This will help you to avoid making expensive mistakes, as will visiting public collections, salerooms and dealers' galleries to assess items. There is also a huge range of specialist authoritative literature on every type of glassware, which is another valuable resource in building up your knowledge. However, the most practical method of learning about glass-ware is to handle it. Fairs, markets, dealers' galleries and auction previews all present opportunities – do not be afraid to pick up pieces and examine them (though always ask if you are in doubt about their fragility), as this will enable you to become familiar with textures, weights, styles and tones or colours, as well as common defects and repairs. Marks or signatures on antique glass are rare, so hands-on experience is one of the most immediate ways of acquainting yourself with the styles of different manufacturers or decorators.

Once you have done a certain amount of homework you will be better prepared to start buying. If you buy to use, always bear in mind that glass should, where possible, be suitable for your lifestyle. Remember that suites of glass tableware – sets of decanters, bowls and glasses in different sizes – though produced only from the early 19thC, are quite rare, often because they were divided among family members as part of a bequest. If you aim to build up table services, you can either concentrate on first acquiring wine glasses – the most practical and widely available element – and then finding, for example, sherry glasses that complement them, or buy

> ### COLLECTOR'S CHECKLIST
> - **BUY WHAT YOU LIKE**
> - **BUY THE BEST YOU CAN**
> - **LEARN ABOUT GLASS FROM BOOKS AND MUSEUMS**
> - **GAIN EXPERIENCE OF HANDLING GLASS BY VISITING AUCTION HOUSES, FAIRS AND ANTIQUES SHOPS**

A magnifying glass, a brush (for cleaning dirty glass), a cloth tube (to absorb condensation) and books on collecting and marks are all useful tools for new collectors.

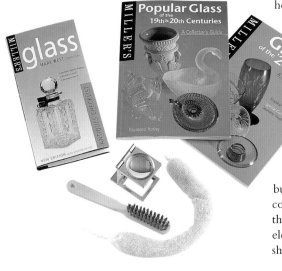

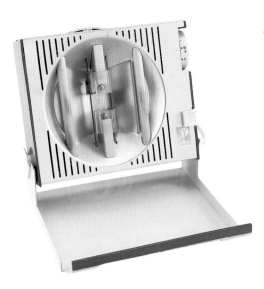

A light machine shows up any impurities and cracks in a glass. The glass is placed on the metal tray, and the light is shone through it to illuminate any faults.

different single glasses of a style that appeals per place setting (i.e. the different glasses for wine, water, champagne etc.)

Collecting "proper" may involve rather more research. A few assorted pieces of glass do not really constitute a collection but are better described as a decorative group – if you find this is more practical, acquire pieces you find attractive and can afford until the space you want to fill is complete. To form a larger collection it is useful to focus on a particular theme, for example a certain glassmaking area or period, colour or decoration. This could be, for example, 18thC drinking glasses, which are characterized by a wide range of decorative stems, 19thC Bohemian glass, or scent bottles. Somewhat rarer and more expensive are early paperweights, American and French art glass and 15th and 16thC glass. Increasing public interest in 20thC design has meant that post-war glass – some of which is highly sculptural – and more practical domesticware such as Pyrex dishes are also becoming collectable. These are among the most affordable types of glass available today. Whatever your budget and tastes, you are likely to find a suitable area. Always buy slowly

and carefully – spend as much as you can afford on good-quality items – the premier rule of collecting. If you have, for example, £1,000 to spend, it might be preferable to buy two fine-quality items at £500 each. Do not attempt to buy "bargains" – there is invariably a reason why an object seems unbelievably inexpensive: usually it is damaged or restored.

When starting out it is advisable to buy from dealers rather than at auctions as instant decisions when bidding are not required. Forming a relationship with a friendly specialist dealer is also invaluable – remember that most dealers will want to help a regular customer. Always keep receipts and up-to-date records of items as you purchase them, to enable you to keep up with the latest market trends and prices, as well as for insurance purposes. Remember that fashion has a certain influence over price – some areas of glass may enjoy increased interest while others will temporarily decline. It is therefore all the more important that you buy pieces that appeal to you – another golden rule of collecting – and if in the long term you make a profit this will be an added bonus.

At the top end of the collecting market are items such as this "Elephant" vase (c.1920) by Emile Gallé, the French maker of Art Nouveau glassware, worth over £20,000/$32,000.

AUCTIONS

Auctions, whether at major houses in large cities or smaller branches in regions, are one of the most stimulating atmospheres in which to buy or sell antique glass, and an ideal environment in which to discover the whole range of glass production. Large auction houses offer spectacular expensive items as well as more modestly priced smaller pieces – mostly in regular sales, divided into age, country of origin or type of ware, or even a notable collection, for example of 18th or 19thC glass or paperweights. Pieces made after 1900, especially those by a notable maker or designer, are often included in more general sales based on 20thC design. Smaller provincial sales and those held by independent auctioneers can offer more scope for buying less expensive pieces in general sales. Specialist publications and directories will list auction houses and auctioneers as well as independent dealers, and so can be useful for contacting them to find out dates and information on sales. All auctions can seem rather daunting at first, but with careful preparation they can be one of the most exciting and useful ways in which to build up your collection.

BUYING AT AUCTION CHECKLIST

- **READ THROUGH THE CATALOGUE CAREFULLY**
- **TAKE YOUR TIME AT THE VIEWING**
- **STICK TO YOUR LIMIT**

CATALOGUES

Most auction houses and salerooms will offer a catalogue (usually for a fee) of a forthcoming sale, available from one month to one week before the sale. Catalogues vary from large illustrated colour publications to simple typed sheets, and list all items for sale (known as "lots") with a number allocated to each lot – sometimes several items are grouped to form one lot, in which case they are described as "multiple lots". Catalogues from the major auction houses should include a description of the object, including the maker or decorator if known, country of origin if known, date or approximate date, type of object, details of provenance if available, marks or signatures if appropriate, and damage or restoration, for example a chipped foot on a drinking glass. Most catalogues include a disclaimer that the descriptions reflect the "opinion" of the cataloguer only, and so are not bound by the Trade Descriptions Act, so recompense is available only if you discover that your cut-glass decanter is a modern reproduction rather than an early 19thC original. An estimated price range is also included in the description of the lot but should only be considered as an approximate guide to the final price that the lot will fetch.

VIEWING

A public viewing of lots takes place in the days before the sale. It is ideal to attend the viewing if you can as this is one of the most fruitful methods of handling and learning about antique glass. Examine the items you

This glass jug has been bought at an auction; the ticket on it gives the date and number of the sale, the lot number of the jug, and the name of the auction house.

are interested in very carefully and make your own decision as to their authenticity, condition and age. Even if the catalogue entry does not specifically mention damage or restoration this does not meant that there is none. Smaller provincial auction viewings may involve sifting through boxes of multiple lots to find the piece or pieces you are interested in buying.

Most sales at larger auction houses will have a specialist responsible for the sale – it is worth consulting him or her if you need more information: for example the expected price (if this is not given in the catalogue), the level of interest shown in that particular lot during the viewing, and other details such as provenance or the technique used to form the object. Condition reports might also be available free of charge. Try to avoid viewing on the morning of the sale as porters in the auction house will be in the process of preparing lots for the auction.

PAYMENT

At the viewing you may find it useful to clarify procedures for bidding and payment. Most large auction houses will require you to register before you bid, by filling in a form with details of your name, address and bank – many smaller salerooms may require your name and address only when you have bid successfully for a lot. In return for registration you will be given a paddle – a piece of card or plastic with a bidding number on it. Also find out whether the auction house accepts credit cards, and whether cheques need to be cleared before you are able to collect your purchase. There may also be a charge for interest and storage if the lot is not paid for and collected within five working days. Set a maximum price that you are prepared to pay – if you are unsure about bidding in person, or you cannot attend the sale, you can leave a bid with a commissions clerk or an auctioneer to bid on your behalf. They are bound to buy as cheaply as they can and will follow your instructions on maximum bids.

It is important to view the items before a sale to ensure that they are in good condition and are genuine pieces; for instance, the cameo glass on this pair of scent bottles by Thomas Webb & Sons should be checked carefully for signs of damage.

BIDDING

Your lot may be at the beginning or the end of the sale – if the latter, check how many lots are likely to be sold before yours, and when you need to arrive at the saleroom. Be disciplined about sticking strictly to your price limit – remember that you will have to pay the auction house commission and VAT on top. At the start of bidding the auctioneer will announce the number of the lot to be sold, and bidding begins just below the lower price indicated in the catalogue. Some lots are given reserve prices to ensure that they are not sold below their value. Attract the auctioneer's attention if you want to join in the bidding at any stage – this may prove more difficult than expected, contrary to popular myths – but remember that the auctioneer may only accept a certain number of bids at any one time, and you may only be able to start bidding if someone else drops out. The bidding rises in increments, usually a percentage of the last bid. If your bid is successful the auctioneer's gavel falls and the bidding stops. The price at which this occurs is known as the hammer price: you will be charged the auction house premium/commission (which can be 10 to 20 per cent of the hammer price) and VAT on the premium.

SELLING

Selling items from your collection at an auction is a fairly straightforward process. Take the piece you would like to sell into the auction house for an over-the-counter valuation for which no charge should be made. There is also no obligation to sell, but remember that some of the larger auction houses may only sell items over a certain value. The specialist giving the valuation may sometimes want to take your item in for further research. The figure he or she quotes will be the hammer price that the item is likely to fetch in a sale – you will be charged commission and VAT on the commission, as well as insurance and handling charges, and sometimes a photography charge if your item is to be illustrated in a catalogue.

AUCTIONS ON THE INTERNET

With the explosion in Internet use, auctions are now appearing on the World Wide Web. Antiques are included in on-line auctions held by some major auction houses, as well as in more general websites; it is strongly advised that you use the former, since the descriptions of the lots and conditions of sale should be similar to those you encounter when bidding in person at a major auction house. The disadvantage of on-line auctions is that you cannot handle the object (although you can usually view an image), so they are only useful when you have built up some experience. However, you can bid for several lots at once, the bidding process is confidential, and you can often quickly find whether there are any items that you are interested in by entering keywords into the website's search facility. Bear in mind that on-line auctions can last for several days or weeks, usually at the discretion of the lot's seller, and are not linked to real-time auctions held in the auction house itself. To bid you will normally need to register your name, contact information and usually a credit card number – in return you will be asked to select a username and password that enables you to bid. Use the search facility, if available, to find the lots you are interested in – each lot

Attending glass sales, such as this one at Phillips in London, is an excellent way for both novice and expert collectors to learn about buying and selling glass.

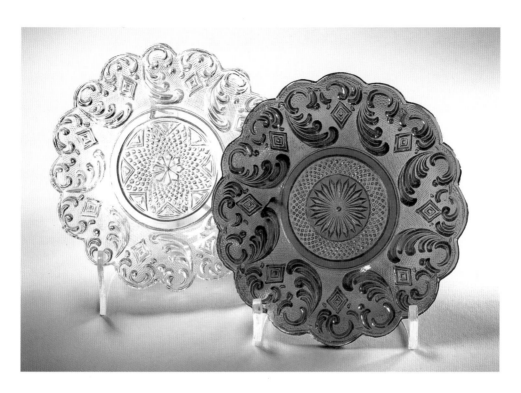

Many of the items that come up for sale at auction are affordable and make good starting points for a new collection, like these cup plates dating from the 1840s.

should have a photograph, a catalogue description and the e-mail address of the seller in case you need to find out more information. If you wish to bid, click on the appropriate button and enter your bid; remember that many on-line auctions of the major auction houses are centred in the USA so prices may be given in dollars. You will be identified to other bidders only by a paddle number (as in normal auctions), and a list of the bids should be given, with the paddle numbers of the other bidders so that you can see how many people are bidding against you. The bidding is carried out using normal increments. If you are unsuccessful you should receive an e-mail saying that you have been outbid, while if you are successful you will be notified that your credit card has been debited with the hammer price, commission, VAT and, if necessary, shipping costs. The expansion of web facilities is likely to lead to new developments in on-line auctions over the next few years, so it is worthwhile checking websites fairly regularly for updates if you are interested in bidding on-line.

ANTIQUES SHOPS, JUNK SHOPS & CHARITY SHOPS

A reputable dealer can be one of the most important factors when you are forming your glass collection. Unlike auctions, where you may need to decide in an instant whether or not to buy, at a dealer's shop you can take your time when deciding what to purchase and how much you are willing to pay for it. Another advantage of buying from a dealer when beginning your collection is that it is likely that he or she will be able to share his or her specialist knowledge of glass with you, to help you to avoid making expensive mistakes.

Visiting a glass shop and speaking to a dealer can be rewarding as he or she will give you advice on what to look out for when collecting glass and will have a wide range of pieces from which you can choose.

> **BUYING FROM DEALERS CHECKLIST**
> - MAKE SURE THAT THE DEALER IS A MEMBER OF A REPUTABLE TRADE BODY
> - TAKE YOUR TIME WHEN DECIDING WHAT TO BUY
> - CHECK WHETHER ANY REPAIRS OR RESTORATION HAVE BEEN CARRIED OUT
> - NEGOTIATE TO GET THE BEST PRICE POSSIBLE
> - GET A DETAILED RECEIPT

There are no specialist qualifications or examinations required for becoming an antiques dealer in Great Britain (though there are in some continental European countries), so the most reliable method of finding a reputable dealer is to contact the two main trade associations: the British Antique Dealers' Association (BADA) and the London and Provincial Antique Dealers' Association (LAPADA). In the USA antiques dealers are represented by the Art and Antique Dealers League of America (AADLA) and the National Antique and Art Dealers Association of America (NAADAA). The logo of one of these organizations displayed in a dealer's shop window indicates that he or she

is registered with the association, has agreed to adhere to a strict code of practice, and has good-quality stock that has been vetted and approved on a regular basis by the association's committee to ensure that the standards required are maintained.

While there are no specialist glass-dealers' associations in the UK, you will find that a wide variety of dealers stock antique glass. These range from general dealers, who may only have a few pieces of glass of varying dates and countries of origin, to specialist dealers who concentrate on, say, European drinking glasses or 20thC studio glass. It is preferable to contact a specialist dealer as he or she is likely to have more expertise in and a greater depth of knowledge of, a particular field of glass. If you are interested in contemporary glass, remember that some galleries or dealers may hold exhibition previews at which you can meet the glass artist in person and therefore gain some valuable insights into his or her work. Also bear in mind that nowadays many dealers have websites on the Internet advertising their stock, some with photographs, descriptions of items available, and prices – but always double-check that the dealer in question is a member of one of the recognized trade associations.

The advantage of building up a good rapport with a dealer is that he or she may be able to help you locate special pieces that you are interested in acquiring. While specialist publications on antiques are a useful source of reference, the accumulated practical and visual knowledge that a dealer builds up over the years is an invaluable aid when you are beginning or developing your collection. Many dealers also offer special payment arrangements for regular clients, and you may be able to take home a piece on approval. When you have decided on a purchase, find out as much as you can about the provenance, date, history, general condition and restoration, if any, of the piece from the dealer. If he or she acquired the piece from a well-known collection or collector this may enhance its value, and it may also be useful to ascertain

This shopfront displays the fine array of antique and modern glass available through specialist dealers; find out which dealer suits your needs most closely.

the significance of any decoration, especially if the piece is commemorative (e.g. an English Jacobite drinking glass), or if there is a mark or signature. When negotiating a price, do not haggle – always ask for the dealer's "best" price, particularly if you are considering buying a group of items. The price of antique glass may often seem higher at a dealer's shop than at auction, but remember that the mark-up on the stock may reflect the cost of repairs, restoration or cleaning at the dealer's expense, while you will also not have to pay the extra costs incurred at auction for the auction house premium. After you have paid for the item, always obtain a full receipt with the date of the purchase, the name and address of the dealer, a description of the item – including the type of object, its country of origin (if known) and date and, most important, any repairs or restoration – and the price paid. While essential for insurance purposes and for keeping accurate records of your collection, a detailed receipt

Always ask for a detailed receipt when buying from a dealer, as this will provide a safeguard against any questions of authenticity or condition once you get the piece of glass home.

can also be useful if there are subsequent problems or disputes over authenticity. Bear in mind that dealers and galleries are covered by the Trade Descriptions Act, so you should be able to obtain a full refund if you find that a decanter advertised as an 18thC original is in fact a modern reproduction. However, you will not be able to obtain a refund if the description of the item as sold was accurate or if you simply change your mind, although some dealers will be willing to exchange the item for one you prefer at a similar price.

JUNK SHOPS AND CHARITY SHOPS

It is possible that you may find a hitherto overlooked glass treasure in a junk shop or charity shop, but do not expect always to find a bargain. Junk shops – usually full of items from house clearances – and charity shops may often contact dealers if they obtain items which they consider might be valuable or

unusual, so you are unlikely, for example, to find a desirable piece of Regency cut glass at an unusually low price. While trawling through the varied items in such shops is not generally efficient for the serious collector, it can be useful for finding more modest pieces on a limited budget – such shops are a good source for finding such items as late 19th or early 20thC single decorated drinking glasses or good-quality modern glass; a modern Waterford glass decanter, for example, that might sell for several hundred pounds when new could be obtained for a fraction of that price in a junk shop. As with dealers, always ask for a receipt, but do not rely on it to give you accurate information as to the maker, the date and, especially, the condition of the piece – always avoid buying pieces that are damaged as, unless they are exceptionally rare, they are unlikely to hold their value and may cost many times the price to restore or repair.

SELLING TO A DEALER

If you consider selling an item from your collection, a dealer's is a good place to begin as, once you have negotiated a price, you will know exactly what you will receive; there are no deductions for seller's commission, insurance or photography as at auction houses, which at first may seem a more immediately attractive proposition owing to well-publicized sales at which some works sell for hundreds of thousands of pounds. The first step is to find a reputable specialist who has expertise in the area of the piece you want to sell, as he or she will be able to give you valuable advice and/or information about the piece even if not wanting to buy it. Telephone to make sure that the person who buys the stock is in, or make an appointment; remember that the buying rather than selling customer are the dealer's priority, and that he or she may be approached to buy stock several

Dealers may be keen to collect certain types of glass, and they are a good place to start if you have an item to sell. You may be able to negotiate a trade-in for a new piece.

times a week. If the item is too fragile and/or too large to carry, you might consider sending a photo or asking the dealer to call at your home. Ask what price he or she might sell the item for, and find out as much as you can (if you did not originally buy it) about its origin, date, maker and condition. Trust the dealer's expertise, but get more than one opinion as you do not have the safeguard of the auction room, where the larger number of potential buyers means that the piece will generally realize its market value even if it is undervalued in the catalogue. Remember that you can also obtain a verbal valuation from an auction house without any obligation to sell.

"KNOCKERS"

It is not advisable to sell to people who call unsolicited at your home or put leaflets through your door asking if you have any antiques for sale. Many of these people are unscrupulous and may try to deceive people, especially the elderly, into selling their property at a fraction of its value.

FAIRS, MARKETS & BOOT SALES

Other venues at which to buy and study antique glass range from large established fairs held at prestigious venues in major cities to smaller, more modest collectors' fairs in church halls. Outdoor markets can also be a fertile hunting ground for less expensive items, but the pieces on display must be viewed with caution, as you will be less dependent on the expertise (and integrity) of the vendor and more on your own judgement.

MAJOR FAIRS

Large annual antiques fairs are advertised in both the national press and specialist publications on antiques. Such fairs can be one of the most valuable places in which to learn about glass, and to familiarize yourself with the particular area of glass in which you are interested, as they present a large number of specialist antiques dealers, often recognized experts, gathered in one place. Stock of very high quality is usually on display, including rare and valuable pieces often seen on the market for the first time; however, you may find that many dealers will also have much lower-priced items available. At such venues you can contact dealers from far afield whom you might not otherwise be able to meet. The range of top-quality items also enables you to compare and contrast items of a similar period or by the same maker, and to make an informed choice, either if you are buying at the fair or subsequently.

There is usually an entrance fee, but this often includes an illustrated catalogue which features details of exhibitors, including their telephone numbers, addresses and e-mail and website information, as well as photographs of their stock or the type of glass in which they specialize; it can also be a useful reference source.

You might also find the names of experts on the "vetting committee" listed in the catalogue –

> **BUYING AT FAIRS, MARKETS & BOOT SALES CHECKLIST**
> - ARRIVE EARLY IN ORDER TO FIND THE BEST BARGAINS
> - COMPARE PRICES BETWEEN STALLS BEFORE BUYING
> - TAKE CASH WITH YOU IF YOU INTEND TO BUY AT A MARKET OR BOOT SALE
> - ALWAYS GET A RECEIPT

exhibitors at many major fairs, and increasingly some smaller ones, are "vetted" by a group of specialists to ensure that the items on offer are authentic and the descriptions of the stock are accurate: mentioning, for example and if appropriate, that a piece is restored. Dateline fairs are those at which stock is vetted to check that items are made before a certain date, e.g. 1900 for Victorian pieces. The fact that a fair is vetted can give the new collector confidence when buying or even just examining items to expand his or her knowledge. If you decide to purchase an item at a fair, all the main points to remember when buying from a dealer apply: you should get a detailed, accurate receipt with a full description of the object, the dealer's contact details, and the price paid.

An antiques fair is an interesting place to view glass of all kinds, from rare and valuable pieces to more commonplace items.

Local antiques fairs and markets are less predictable in the items that are for sale. There may be some bargains, but exercise caution, especially when purchasing an "antique".

SMALLER FAIRS

Smaller antiques and collectors' fairs are held throughout the country, and are usually advertised in the local press. The disadvantage of such fairs is that the dealers are likely to be part-time or retired enthusiasts, rather than full-time professionals, with much less comprehensive stock than at larger fairs. These fairs are generally good places to find modern pieces or collectables, such as miscellaneous items of tableware. The objects on show are not usually vetted, even though some fairs might be advertised as such, so you should use your own judgement when checking dates, restoration and authenticity. You can usually obtain a receipt, but it will not always be as detailed as one you would get at a major fair from a reputable dealer. As at larger fairs, you should be able to pay by cheque or credit card, but some dealers at smaller venues may want to clear a cheque before releasing larger or more valuable pieces.

MARKETS

Street markets are held worldwide, with a wide range of stallholders, but some dealers are less than reputable, so be on your guard against purchasing stolen goods – it is essential to get a written receipt as it shows that you bought in good faith. You will also need to be an early bird, as you will find that some dealers have arrived first and bought the best pieces. Despite the generally low prices, you will usually find that most pieces are not in good condition and will need some restoration – beware particularly of chipped or cloudy glass.

BOOT SALES

These attract some regular, semi-professional and not always reputable dealers, so you are unlikely to find a rare item in good condition. You will need to make up your own mind as to the authenticity of an object or if it has been restored. It can also be very difficult to get a reliable receipt, so note carefully where and when you bought a piece; also check carefully for counterfeit notes and beware of pickpockets.

PART 2

CARE & SECURITY

ABOVE BOHEMIAN AND FRENCH GILDED DECANTERS,
LEFT: £750–800/$1,200–1,275;
RIGHT: £180–200/$290–325.

LEFT A DRAMATIC DISPLAY OF FRENCH
VASELINE GLASS.

CARE & RESTORATION

Though a brittle material, glass will last a lifetime in good condition if cleaned, handled and stored carefully, using a few straight-forward guidelines. Even though it will break when dropped, glass tableware in particular was designed to be functional, and 19th and 20thC pieces are often surprisingly robust and suitable for everyday domestic use. However, rare and valuable glass from the 16thC and 17thC often requires specialist attention, as early glass recipes were sometimes chemically unstable and resulted in "crizzling". This refers to a fine network of small cracks on the surface of the glass owing to an excess of alkali in the batch, which leaches out and crystallizes, creating tiny fissures. Such "diseased" glass continues to deteriorate, as the process causing crizzling cannot be reversed.

> **CARE & RESTORATION CHECKLIST**
> - ALWAYS USE A PROFESSIONAL RESTORER FOR REPAIRS
> - TAKE GREAT CARE WHEN CLEANING GLASS
> - STORE ITEMS CAREFULLY

CLEANING

Most glass can be cleaned simply by using warm, soapy water and a soft cloth, fine brush or sponge. Avoid very hot water as this will raise the temperature of the glass and weaken the body if it is cooled quickly: this is known as "thermal shock" and can lead to cracks. Always handle the object with care when cleaning to avoid breaking handles, rims and feet. Large hollow vessels such as decanters or jugs should be cleaned with a bottle brush, and bleach will remove stubborn wine or spirit stains. However, an object such as a decanter or vase with a cloudy appearance on the inside needs to be cleaned by a specialist, since this is an indication that water has etched the surface of the glass. Never use bleach or detergent on enamelled or gilded glass as both are likely to damage the delicate paint or layer of gold. Abrasive cleaners should also be avoided, as they will leave fine scratches on the surface. After cleaning, the glass object should always be rinsed, and dried with a soft cloth, gently but thoroughly to prevent water stains. Decanters, vases and jugs can be dried by being left upside down in a dry warm atmosphere, for example an airing cupboard. Do not put glass on a very cold or hot surface directly after washing as this may also cause thermal shock and weaken the glass body. Never put antique glass or any other good glass in a dishwasher as the detergents used have a high concentration of phosphates, which cause lead glass to cloud and will leave spots or rings on soda glass; some dishwasher detergent crystals may also abrade the surface.

STORAGE AND HANDLING

Always take great care in handling glass because of its fragility, but do not be afraid to pick it up and examine it as this is the best method of familiarizing yourself with its

Some glassware is more prone to damage than others: the swag decoration on this Venetian vase (late 1920s) has a piece missing, reducing its value to a tenth of the original price.

weight, texture and colour. However, avoid over-handling painted and gilded glass as the delicate surface decoration is likely to wear off easily; this also applies to crizzled glass, which is exceptionally fragile, and ancient glass with an iridescent surface that may be damaged by the acid left in fingerprints. To prevent breakage, handle items such as sets of drinking glasses one at a time – do not attempt to lift a whole group with one hand. Lift large and heavy objects such as bowls with both hands to stabilize the weight, and never pick up decanters or jugs by their handle only, as the join between handle and body is vulnerable. Chinking glasses together or tapping them roughly may also lead to cracks – these may appear very small at first but will always run. Most glass is best stored in dry, airtight display cases, although some early glass needs to be kept in conditions of controlled temperature and humidity to prevent crizzling – consult an expert if in doubt. Dry conditions are particularly important – remember that water can damage the surface of glass and leave stains as much as other liquids. Avoid stacking too many items, even flat pieces such as plates, as the weight of the top pieces will put a strain on those underneath; there should also be enough space between each object to ensure safe handling. Low-voltage halogen lights are the best way of lighting a display case as strong lights will provide too much heat, raising the temperature of the glass and making it vulnerable to thermal shock.

RESTORATION

One of the most important points to remember when you begin to collect is to avoid buying damaged pieces, as these are always less desirable than those in good condition. When buying, always examine items carefully to check for cracks and chips which are often not immediately visible. If you have a damaged item it is best to take it to a specialist glass restorer; do not attempt to repair an item at home as you may make the damage worse and render the piece useless and/or valueless. Good glass restorers can be

Heavily gilded and enamelled pieces, such as this bowl of 1871 by Philippe-Joseph Brocard, must be cleaned with great care: bleach and detergent will damage the delicate surface.

found by word of mouth or through a reputable dealer.

As glass tableware has often been heavily used, the most common form of damage is chipping. A good glass restorer can polish out small chips in, for example, the rim of a drinking glass – in 19th and 20thC glass such repairs should not adversely affect the value. However, such repairs should be avoided for earlier glass or more elaborate pieces such as cameo glass as they will affect the price if the item is resold. Museum restorers use transparent colourless acrylic, polyester or epoxy resins to fill in missing areas, but this method is not practical for everyday items as it is expensive and not permanent. A restorer can use transparent glues and adhesives to replace such elements as handles that have broken off. While the join will still be visible – owing to the transparency and smooth surface of glass – the item will be usable.

Coloured glass is virtually impossible to restore – the metallic oxides now used to colour glass bodies are different from those used in antique glass and can never produce exactly the same tone, especially for green glassware. Gilding is costly and difficult to repair, so it is advisable to leave worn gold gilding as the brighter tone and slightly grainy texture of regilding always show. Silver mounts, often attached to 19thC claret jugs with plaster of Paris, are also difficult to remove and replace.

DISPLAY

A fine display of antique glass can enhance the attractiveness of a room – the sparkling brilliance of cut-glass tableware and lighting fixtures will reflect and catch the light, while coloured glass can complement a furnishing scheme. It is always advisable to display your collection in a way that suits your lifestyle – for example, do not leave drinking glasses or decanters on a table if you use it for working on. More than any other material, glass is susceptible to breakage and should always be kept out of reach, especially from children, to avoid accidental damage – remember also that fragments of broken glass can be razor sharp.

There are two main alternatives when considering the display of your collection – you may want to keep items in a cabinet for visual display only, or you may also want to take them out and use them, for example using drinking glasses for dinner parties. If you prefer the former it is best to store items in a glass-fronted airtight and dry display cabinet so that the glass is not exposed to dust. Where possible it is preferable to have purpose-built cupboards that complement your existing furnishing scheme rather than a ready-made display case. Glass is always best displayed on glass, so fit your cabinet with glass shelves – acrylic display stands or cases are also useful, but the soft acrylic surface can easily be scratched by glass. Low-voltage halogen lights are the most suitable method of lighting, and should be located directly underneath or above the objects to minimize shadows and reflections. Paperweights – designed to be viewed from above – can be attractively displayed in glass-topped specimen tables.

> **DISPLAYING YOUR GLASS COLLECTION CHECKLIST**
> ● CHOOSE A METHOD OF DISPLAY THAT IS APPROPRIATE TO YOUR HOME AND LIFESTYLE AS WELL AS YOUR GLASSWARE
> ● AVOID DISPLAYING YOUR COLLECTION IN A WAY THAT WILL ATTRACT UNWANTED ATTENTION FROM THOSE PASSING BY THE HOUSE

It is advisable to present glass items that you intend to use fairly regularly on a sturdy cabinet, sideboard or table so that they are less subject to vibration, and consequently less liable to chipping or breakage by being knocked together. Avoid grouping too many items – a single bowl or vase is often adequate to enhance a table. Mirrors placed behind items such as decanters on a tray will also complement glass. Never use wire holders to hang glass plates on a wall as these will exert too much pressure on the body, causing cracks and chips; the best method of displaying these is on a stand of an appropriate size and shape, with adequate support.

This selection of Victorian tableware makes an attractive display as well as being easily accessible for use at a dinner party or formal occasion.

Pieces of coloured glass can be displayed particularly effectively on glass shelves fixed across a landing window where the light falls obliquely. Avoid mixing too many items of more than one shade or colour and/or plain and engraved or cut glass. An arrangement of small groups of glass items is often more attractive than rows of pieces of the same shape, type and size, which might look altogether too much like a display in a shop; decanters and tazzas, for example, can make a useful focus around which smaller items can be arranged. Too many items grouped together will also reduce the amount of light falling on each object and make the display dark.

Follow a few simple rules to keep your display of glass in good condition. Though glass is enhanced by light, do not display it in direct strong light, either sunlight or artificial, as this will lead to a rise in the temperature of the glass body, possibly causing thermal stresses that may result in cracks. Coloured glass in particular should not be displayed in strong sunlight as chemicals in the body may cause crizzling. While an attractive bunch of flowers will complement a glass vase, do not leave vases filled with water for too long as the water will corrode the surface, leaving a cloudy appearance. Similarly, do not store wine or spirits in decanters or claret jugs for excessively long periods, as alcohol will also leave stains, though it is safe to use them for dinner parties, for example. It has also been said that lead will leach out from lead glass into liquid stored in decanters – this does happen, but extremely slowly over a period of many years, and in very small amounts. Always clean out wine glasses after use, and rinse and dry them thoroughly.

Decanter stoppers should always be dried thoroughly after use as otherwise they may become jammed in the top of the decanter. Do not let candles burn too far down glass candlesticks and candelabra, or the candle stub can be very difficult to remove; it should not be taken out with a knife or other sharp implement as this will scratch the glass – instead pour a little warm water around the

This display of a collection of etched, painted, gilded, jewelled and cut glass is a good example of how glassware can be shown to best advantage within the home.

top of the rim and the wax will soften, making it easy to dislodge. Take particular care when handling or displaying paperweights; if knocked they can "bruise" (but not crack) inside, causing permanent damage and thus reducing their value. Also be careful when arranging jugs as the handles are vulnerable to breakage.

SECURITY

Glass is a relatively secure form of collecting: unlike silver, jewellery or watches, the most widely collected items are of relatively low value. It is also less portable, as it requires careful handling and wrapping. However, it is always important to ensure that your collection is adequately protected and insured because of the increasing risk of theft. Remember that glass should always be stored carefully as it is particularly susceptible to accidental damage if a burglary occurs.

INSURANCE & VALUATIONS

The type of insurance required depends on the nature of your collection. If you collect small valuable items for investment, especially glass

> ### KEEPING YOUR GLASS SAFE CHECKLIST
> - DISPLAY YOUR GLASS WITH GREAT CARE
> - MAKE SURE THAT YOUR COLLECTION IS INSURED TO AN APPROPRIATE VALUE
> - PHOTOGRAPH YOUR ITEMS
> - KEEP FULL UP–TO–DATE RECORDS IN CASE OF THEFT

made before the 19th century, you could consider putting them in a bank safety deposit box, though check the cost as fees may increase annually and outweigh the value of your collection. If the value of your collection is less than about £50,000/$80,000 it can often be included as part of your general household contents insurance. Glass tableware in particular is often used regularly, so it may be wiser to insure it up to its full retail replacement value – specialist antiques insurers might also have lower premiums than general insurance companies. The insurance value should also reflect the costs you would have to pay if you chose to replace stolen or missing items at auction or through an independent dealer. You should always follow the insurance company's stipulations exactly, as otherwise it may be difficult or impossible to replace your property in the event of loss.

Most insurance companies will require a written valuation of your collection. This should be carried out by an auction house – often with experts in the field – or a specialist valuer or reputable dealer. It is advisable to choose a valuer who has a specialist knowledge of the field in which you collect, as he or she may be able to help you to locate or replace the objects from your collection if they go missing. An auction house or a dealer will not charge for an informal valuation if you take along one or two objects to be valued but you will have to pay for a written one. Costs vary widely, so it is worth investigating to compare prices, which can be charged either as a fixed daily fee – a well-qualified valuer should be able to assess about 100–300 pieces a day – or as a percentage of the sum insured. The former option is often the less expensive one if you only have a small collection. A written valuation should always

Extremely valuable items, such as this leaded-glass and bronze Tiffany table lamp (c.1906), worth over £10,000/ $16,000, must be well insured against theft and damage.

Those fortunate enough to own an antique chandelier, such as this Irish Georgian piece from *c*.1800, should be careful not to display it too conspicuously to the outside world.

collection as this is the best way of recovering stolen property. Keep detailed records of each item – these should include the date and location of the purchase, the price charged and whether you paid in cash, by cheque or by using a credit card, as well as the dimensions and decorative features – and also make a note of any signatures, defects, chips, cracks and repairs. If there is an engraved inscription or a motto, copy the words out in full. Marker pens should not be used on glass as the ink will wear if the object is used and washed regularly.

It is also vital to photograph each item in your collection individually against a plain background in natural light – do not use a flash. Detailed shots of inscriptions or decoration can also help in identifying the object if it is stolen, while general shots of a table with settings for a dinner party, for example, may enable you to distinguish your property in a similar setting. Keep one set of photographs in a secure place and another with the records of your collection. Missing items can be traced by using the Art Loss Register, a national computer database containing details of stolen property to which dealers, auctioneers and insurance companies subscribe – the cost of including a stolen piece is relatively low. An advertisement in a specialist publication, such as the *Antiques Trade Gazette* or *Trace* in Britain, or the *Maine Antiques Digest* in the US, may also be useful in finding missing items.

be acceptable to the insurer and should include a full description of each piece: the type of object, date or approximate date, dimensions, weight, decoration, any defects or repairs and value for insurance purposes. A written valuation should be updated every four years as market prices change.

RECORDS

It is extremely important to keep up-to-date and accurate records of all the pieces in your

SECURITY IN THE HOME

Although you should always be able to enjoy and admire your collection by putting it on display in your home, it is important to exercise a certain amount of discretion – do not hang large and expensive antique chandeliers in a living room with no curtains, for example. Take precautions with the security of your home – advice can be obtained by consulting a crime prevention officer from your local police station. It is also useful to have locks on all doors and windows, security lights and an alarm, which may also reduce your insurance premiums.

PART 3

THE BASICS

ABOVE A HYACINTH-BULB VASE,
c.1860, £100–150/$160–240.

LEFT A DETAIL OF A BRITISH ARMORIAL SERVICE
BY THE WEAR FLINT GLASS WORKS
c.1830, £400–600/$650–950.

TYPES OF GLASS

Glass has been used over the centuries for an extraordinarily wide range of decorative and functional objects, from simple, disposable bottles to elaborate cut-glass vessels, mirrors and large panes for windows and architectural cladding. It is one of the most common materials in everyday use, but until relatively recently was regarded as a luxury commodity, and as a substitute for precious or semi-precious stones. Glass was first made in the 3rd millennium BC in the Middle East; some of the earliest glass objects are decorative beads made in ancient Egypt, while production of hollow glass vessels, for expensive oils and perfumes, began there about 1500 BC.

MATERIALS

Glass is a transparent or translucent substance made by fusing silica, derived from sand, quartz or flint, with an alkaline in the form of sodium carbonate (soda) derived from plants, or potassium carbonate (potash) obtained from burnt beechwood, oak or bracken, at high temperature. This combination of ingredients – the basic materials of glassmaking – is known as a "batch". Lime, obtained from chalk or limestone, is usually added as a stabilizer, while small amounts of other ingredients, such as lead or borax, will affect the physical properties of the glass, such as its brilliance. In ancient Rome, cullet (fragments of recycled glass) was added to the batch as a flux to reduce the melting point. Glass is described as a "super-cooled liquid" as it is cooled to a rigid state without crystallization – heating reconverts it to a liquid form. When molten, it is described as "metal", and it is this that is drawn, blown or shaped by the glassmaker. Some glass is also found in nature: black glass (obsidian), formed by volcanic activity, has been used by native Americans to make carvings and tools. Almost pure silica glass is produced in small quantities when lightning strikes a desert, as the desert sand melts under the immense electrical energy discharged and solidifies. The three main types of glass found today are soda-lime, potash and lead glass.

SODA GLASS

Soda glass was the earliest type of glass; in its simplest form it comprises only silica and soda, but this mixture is not durable and will dissolve in water to form a syrupy liquid known as water glass – now commonly used for commercial fireproofing and as a sealant. The addition of lime in small quantities, usually 10 per cent lime to 15 per cent soda and 75 per cent silica, stabilizes the batch and makes the material workable. Soda glass has a short working life – it hardens quickly when cooling – so the amount of soda is often increased. It is generally bubbly in appearance, with a slightly greenish colour, as pictured above; thin and fragile when blown, it is difficult to engrave or cut. Soda glass is still the most common type of glass, used today to make inexpensive, disposable items such as bottles and lightbulbs.

From the beginnings of glassmaking there were attempts to perfect a manmade clear glass imitating natural rock crystal. By the end of the 15thC the Venetians had developed an almost transparent, ductile and durable type of soda glass called *cristallo*, made with the ashes of barilla, a saltwater marsh plant, as a flux, and refined using magnesium oxide. This was used for luxury tazzas, bowls and goblets.

POTASH GLASS

Potash glass is particularly associated with northern and central Europe. Glassmaking was introduced into these areas during Roman Imperial rule, and at first soda glass made with the ashes of marine plants imported from the Mediterranean was produced. By the 10thC, however, northern and central European glassmakers had begun to use potassium-rich ashes (potash) of beechwood, oak and ferns/bracken found in local forests as a flux. This type of glass, characterized by a yellowish-green or brownish colour, due to impurities in the raw materials, was therefore known in German-speaking countries as *Waldglas* (forest glass) and in France as *verre de fougère* (fern glass). A thick, hard glass, potash glass has a longer working life than soda glass but is unsuitable for cutting, and is therefore usually decorated with applied prunts or trailing, as seen on the *Roemer* above. By the late 17thC, following experiments to produce glass imitating natural rock crystals, Bohemian glassmakers had perfected a fine-quality clear potash glass by adding lime, in the form of chalk or limestone, to the batch. This potash-lime glass, as it was known, was more robust than earlier types, with greater brilliance, and could be blown to a sufficient thickness to be cut and wheel-engraved.

LEAD GLASS

The dominance of the English glass industry in the 18thC and early 19thC was largely the result of the invention of lead-oxide glass by the English glassmaker George Ravenscroft in 1673. The addition of red lead (lead oxide) to the batch significantly increased the working life of the glass and its density, making it more brilliant: hence the common description "lead crystal". It is soft but also strong, making it particularly suitable for decorating by cutting and engraving. The main ingredients are three parts silica, two parts red lead and one part potash, plus saltpetre, arsenic and borax. Lead glass is sometimes described as "flint glass" because the earliest examples were made with silica derived from English flints rather than imported Venetian pebbles. It has a distinctive grey tone, as seen below, and is much heavier than soda glass.

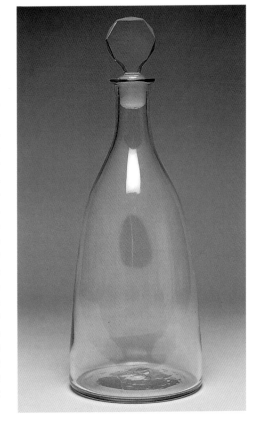

FORMING TECHNIQUES

A variety of methods have been used for forming glass objects: the most familiar type is free blowing, but molten glass can also be cast like metal or shaped in a mould, or, for small hollow vessels, wound round a core.

CASTING

Casting glass in a mould was first used in ancient Mesopotamia around 700 BC for producing statuettes, jars and bowls, and was adapted from casting methods used by potters and metalworkers. Molten glass is poured into a mould and allowed to cool, then the mould is broken away. A perfect cast is difficult to produce, especially for large objects, as the outer layers of the glass cool more rapidly than the inside, and the cast must be cooled slowly in an annealing furnace to prevent permanent stresses inside the material. A type of richly translucent cast glass, known as *pâte-de-verre* (glass paste), was used by French glass artists in the late 19thC and early 20thC. The glass resembled hardstones; the method of production involved packing glass powder coloured with metal oxides into a mould and then firing it at high temperature.

CORE-FORMING

Prior to the invention of glass blowing, most small hollow vessels were produced by core-forming, developed in Egypt about 1650 BC. A core of sand, clay or dung is fixed to a metal rod and moulded into the required shape, then dipped into molten glass or wound with molten glass threads. The rod is then reheated and rolled (marvered) on a flat surface to make walls of

This core-formed translucent amber-brown Egyptian *alabastron* (small bottle) has unusual colouring, as Egyptian glass is more commonly bright, opaque blue.

even thickness. Threads of different coloured glass were often trailed over the surface and combed into contrasting feather-like patterns. After the rim, handle and feet were added, the object was cooled, the metal rod removed and the core scraped out. The process meant that core-forming was only practical for small bottles, flasks and vases.

FREE-BLOWING

Free-blowing is often regarded as the most significant development in the history of glassmaking. Invented in the late 1stC BC in the Middle East under Roman rule, it was the most common method of forming glass until automated pressing was introduced in the 19thC. A process requiring very great skill and dexterity, free-blowing is usually carried out by a team comprising a master craftsman (the gaffer), responsible for forming and working the object, and a number of assistants (the servitors). The basic tool required is a hollow metal pipe (blowing iron) about 1.2m (4ft) long, with a mouthpiece at one end; the other end of the pipe is dipped into a crucible containing molten glass in the furnace to collect a "gather" or small amount of molten glass. The gather is rolled against a paddle or metal plate to cool it slightly, and the gaffer blows into the pipe to expand the gather into a bubble (parison). The finished object is created by alternately blowing the glass and reheating it in a special furnace, called a "glory hole", to restore its malleability, while tools such as shears, tongs (pucellas) and pincers are used to refine the form and to manipulate additional applied gathers into handles, feet, stems and rims. This finishing is often carried out in a

Dating from the 1st-4thC AD, this free-blown Roman tear bottle would have been used to store cosmetics or perfumes.

"glassmaker's chair" – a bench to which horizontal arms are attached, along which the iron is rolled to keep the gather an even shape – the gaffer may also swing the rod to and fro for the same reason. To create drinking glasses, dishes, bowls and other vessels, the parison is transferred while still hot to a solid iron rod called a pontil iron, applied opposite the blowpipe, which is then removed with the waste glass. The open end is drawn out and fashioned into the required shape. After forming, the object is gradually cooled to room temperature - known as annealing – in a lehr. When the pontil is cracked off, a "pontil mark" is often visible: on glass made before the 19thC the pontil was simply snapped off, leaving a rough surface, but later the mark was machine-polished or ground out. Free-blown wares have slight striations on the surface where the object was formed and tooled by hand.

MOULD-BLOWING

Mould-blowing is similar to free-blowing but involves shaping a gather by blowing it into a hinged wooden or metal mould. The technique was introduced by Roman glassmakers during the early 1stC AD. It is useful for producing wares of a uniform size or diameter, such as decanters, and for objects too complex to be formed by core-forming or free-blowing. Two main methods are used:

The simple method of blowing a gather into a shaped mould was used to produce the bowl of this rummer (c.1790–1800) – relatively inexpensive compared with cut glass.

either blowing a gather into a part-mould and then removing it and free-blowing it further to expand the shape or impressed pattern, or blowing a gather into a whole mould to shape an entire object.

PRESS-MOULDING

These two lidded pots (c.1850) have been press-moulded by the Boston & Sandwich Glass Company; the process was very popular in the United States in the 19thC.

A method of pressing molten glass into a patterned mould was developed in ancient Roman times for relief plaques and later used by medieval Islamic craftsmen to make weights and seals. Press-moulding only came into widespread use when the demand for inexpensive, mass-produced patterned glassware increased enormously during the 19thC. The method involves dropping a gather of hot glass into a base mould, then pressing with a plunger attached to the top part of the mould to ensure that molten glass flows into the form and detail of the mould. The mould is often patterned to create a decorative relief design on the object. The technique was patented by various firms in the 1820s, especially in the USA, where the first automated presses using compressed air were developed, rapidly followed by France. Pieces of glass with extremely complicated patterns can be produced by press-moulding, either with a machine or by hand, although the definition is not as good as on original cut glass. The earliest dated pieces of pressed glass in England are commemorative pieces made to mark Queen Victoria's accession and coronation.

DECORATION

Three main categories of decorative technique have been used to embellish glass through the centuries: colouring, incising and applied ornament. Colouring encompasses the addition of metallic oxides to the batch to produce a uniform colour throughout the finished article, as well as the layering of clear and coloured glass through casing and overlay, and the insertion of coloured glass rods in a section of clear glass to produce a variety of ornamental twisting or interlaced patterns, the latter technique associated particularly with Venetian glassmakers. Most glassware can also withstand engraving, and, in the case of heavier lead glass, cutting. These techniques were practised to the highest degree of skill in northern and central Europe from the 17thC. Decoration can also be applied to the surface of glass by trailing, combing and milling, enamelling and gilding.

METALLIC OXIDES

Coloured glass has sometimes been produced accidentally owing to impurities in the batch, in particular those found in coastal sand, but most coloured glass has been produced intentionally by the addition to the batch of metallic oxides, which dissolve in the hot liquid glass and disperse throughout it. Different metals will produce different colours, but the shade will vary according to the amount of metallic oxide used and other additives in the batch.

Blue is the easiest colour to achieve, while yellow and orange are the most complex. It can also be very difficult to match green glass, even pieces made at the same time in one glasshouse, as the tone varies from yellowish-green to a deep rich emerald or olive green. Coloured glass has often been used to imitate hardstones – "mosaic glass", made by arranging thin slices of fused glass rods of different colours in a mould, was invented by ancient Roman glassmakers, while lithyalin glass was a type of marbled coloured glass perfected by the Bohemian glassmaker Friedrich Egermann (1777–1864) in the early 19thC and patented in 1829.

CASING & OVERLAY

Casing and overlay involve fusing one layer of transparent or translucent glass to another: cased glass refers to a clear glass layer over a coloured body, while overlay is the reverse, although the two terms are now interchangeable. An outer vessel is partially blown and placed in a mould, and a second gather of clear or a contrasting colour is placed inside and blown into it, so that the layers fuse and expand together. The process is laborious and complex as different colours of glass cool at different rates, making the object susceptible to cracking when annealed. The best examples of casing are sometimes cut or engraved to reveal the contrasting colour underneath, as seen in the glass below, while opaque layers on paperweights were often cut with facets or "printies" to show the design within. Casing and overlay can be distinguished from flashing or staining by the

much thicker layers: the greatest number of layers is four, otherwise the object becomes opaque.

FLASHING & STAINING

Flashing describes a technique of dipping a glass vessel into a gather of another colour, leaving a very thin surface layer that can be engraved. It was frequently used as a less expensive alternative to cased glass. Staining refers to a method of brushing the surface of the glass with pigments of various colours to create a pictorial or decorative design. In the Middle Ages silver chloride, producing a yellow stain, was painted into glass panes for use in stained-glass windows. The technique was used on decorative glass from the early 19thC.

COLOUR TWISTS

Colour twists are made by embedding one or more rods of coloured or white glass within a clear glass gather and pulling and twisting it to create a spiralling pattern. Inspired by 16thC Venetian *latticinio* glass, this type of decoration is associated particularly with stems on mid-18thC English drinking glasses. Opaque white stems are sometimes described as "cotton" twists; red and green are the colours most commonly found in colour-twist stems, while blue, purple, canary yellow and other intense colours are rarely seen, and are therefore sought after, as are twists of more than one colour.

LATTIMO & LATTICINIO

Lattimo (milk glass), shown above top, is a slightly translucent opaque glass developed in Italy in the 15thC as a porcelain substitute; similar glass was made in Germany, The Netherlands, Bohemia and England in the 18thC. Pure *lattimo* wares are rare, but it was often combined with clear glass in Italy from the early 16thC. The resulting wares, known as *latticinio* or *latticino*, incorporate a variety of interlacing patterns of *lattimo* embedded in a clear glass body (see above). Simple patterns of straight or spiral threads are described as *vetri a filigrana* or *vetri a filato*, while complex, mesh-like patterns are called *vetri a reticello*.

ENGRAVING
DIAMOND-POINT

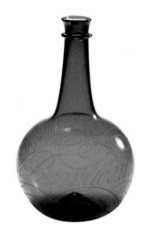

In diamond-point engraving a design can be lightly scratched on the surface of the glass with a stylus tipped with a tiny diamond. The technique was popularized by *façon de Venise* glassmakers in the 16thC and by Bohemian and, especially, Dutch craftsmen in the 17thC and 18thC. It is less laborious and requires less skill than wheel-engraving, so designs are rarely as detailed and were sometimes executed freehand by talented amateurs rather than special engravers. The overall effect is also much more linear than wheel-engraving, and the incised areas are much shallower. As the use of styluses required relatively light pressure on the body of the glass, this method of engraving was suitable for brittle soda glass.

WHEEL

A method of decorating glass surfaces using abrasive discs was first developed in the 1stC AD and was derived from techniques used for engraving gems and hardstones. The object to be engraved is held under the wheel and the surface incised by rotating copper (now composition) discs and an abrasive paste (usually oil combined with emery) – the discs are often of progressive fineness, to add detail to the pattern. The finest exponents of wheel engraving were central European craftsmen from the 16thC to the 18thC, who used a fine-quality potash glass; lead glass is also especially suited to this type of decoration.

Wheel engraving is usually classified in two ways – *hochschnitt*, where design is cut in relief so that it protrudes slightly above the surface, and *tiefschnitt*, in which the pattern is cut into the surface. Most engraved surfaces are left matt to enhance the effect of light and shadow, but in rock-crystal engraving, developed in the 19thC, deeply engraved areas are polished to imitate carved rock crystal.

STIPPLE

Stipple engraving, similar to diamond-point engraving but much more skilled and time-consuming, involves tapping a diamond-pointed needle against the surface of the glass with a light hammer to produce patterns of tiny dots – light areas are dense with dots, while darker areas have fewer. This type of engraving can be identified by the very delicate designs and indented matt surface, and was particularly suitable for thin-walled vessels. It is associated particularly with 17thC glass from The Netherlands, where it was introduced in the early 1620s.

ACID-ETCHING

Acid-etching, a technique probably derived from printmaking, was introduced commercially during the 19thC as an inexpensive alternative to laborious hand engraving. The glass is covered with a resist – an acid-proof coating such as wax or resin – and the design cut through using a pointed stylus; the object is then dipped into hydrofluoric acid, and a matt design is created by the acid dissolving the surface of the glass where it has been

left exposed. The depth of the design depends on how long the object is immersed in the acid.

CAMEO

Like engraving, the technique of cameo glass, perfected in ancient Rome, is derived from lapidary work. An outer layer of cased or flashed glass, usually opaque white, is cut back to reveal the layer of a contrasting colour underneath. The best known example of cameo glass is the Portland Vase (1stC BC– 1stC AD), but the technique was rediscovered during the 19thC after the Portland Vase was brought to England. Cameo glass is usually found on decorative wares such as vases and scent bottles. Some cameos, known as faux or commercial cameos, were acid-cut, using a

similar method to acid-etching; these can be distinguished from hand-carved pieces by the textured background and less defined edges of the design.

CUTTING

The fashion for heavily cut glass reached its peak during the late 18thC and early 19thC in England and Ireland, where lead glass – the most suitable type for cutting – was invented. Glass cutting, like engraving, requires a high level of skill and was usually undertaken by specialist craftsmen. The object is held above the wheel, and iron or stone discs are used to create facets or deep grooves, which are then polished to create a brilliant sparkling surface. A variety of complex cutting patterns, such as strawberry and relief diamonds, developed during the Regency period, though from the 1820s and 1830s simpler, flat-cut vertical facets became more fashionable. During the 1840s bold, simple designs, often incorporating a "Gothic" arch framing heavy-cut diamonds, were in vogue.

ENAMELLING

Glass can be painted with either lacquer or oil paints, or more usually enamel paint. Lacquer and oils are often applied to the reverse of an object, as they cannot be fired and will easily wear off if the object is handled too much. Enamel paints, comprising finely ground glass mixed with metallic oxides in an oily medium, can be painted onto the surface and fired in a low-temperature kiln to fuse the colours to the object. Transparent black, brown and/ or red enamels, known as *Schwarzlot*, were popular from the mid-17thC to the mid-18thC on German and Bohemian

glass. This type of decoration was usually undertaken by *Hausmaler* (home painters) – specialist freelance artists who also frequently decorated porcelain pieces using the same technique.

GILDING

Various methods, using gold leaf or paint, can be used to gild glass. Gilding is sometimes combined with coloured enamels and is often applied to an engraved surface to protect the gold from wear.

Honey gilding involves painting on a mixture of ground gold leaf and honey and firing it at a low temperature to fix the gold. Mercury gilding, which was also used on silver, is a similar process using gold combined with mercury which, when the object is fired, will

burn off leaving a film of gold. This method is, however, no longer used because of the toxicity of the mercury fumes. Cold gilding is a less durable method than either honey or mercury gilding because the gold leaf is mixed with oil and applied to the surface but not fired, so it can easily flake off.

ZWISCHENGOLDGLAS

Zwischengoldglas ("gold between glass") was used on German and Bohemian beakers and tankards during the mid-18thC. Heraldic designs (as above), hunting scenes and religious subjects were popular. Gold or sometimes silver leaf was applied to a clear glass object, sometimes engraved with a pictorial or decorative design or combined with enamel colours, and a tightly fitting outer vessel or "sleeve" of clear glass was placed over the top. *Zwischengoldglas* plaques were also inserted into plain goblets and beakers. Examples of *Zwischengoldglas* are relatively rare, as the application of a sleeve could easily rub off the delicate gold leaf underneath.

SILVER MOUNTS

Silver or silver-gilt mounts have been used widely on glass as handles and lids, especially in the 18thC and 19thC. Most silver-mounted objects found today are scent bottles or wine and claret jugs from the late 19thC. Silver mounts were often secured using plaster of Paris, so they are difficult to replace if they become damaged or worn. The hallmarks on the silver are a valuable method of dating glass.

OTHER METHODS

Glass can also be decorated and manipulated with a variety of tools while still hot.

TRAILING & COMBING

Trailing refers to the application of thin rods of molten glass around the vessel to create a spiralling pattern, and is found especially on pieces of ancient Roman glass and Art Deco-style glass.

Coloured trails can be "combed" into feather-like patterns with a pointed instrument and then marvered to roll them into the surface. This technique was first used on ancient Egyptian core-formed vessels.

Pincering is a method of squeezing or nipping trails or other decorations to create a frilled edge.

PRUNTS

Prunts are blobs of molten glass, usually found on the stems of German drinking vessels such as *Roemer,* and are either left plain or impressed to form textured "raspberry" prunts. Early medieval "claw beakers" feature a drawn-out prunt, one end of which is fused to another part of the vessel.

LAMPWORK

The ornately tooled "wings" of 15thC and 16thC Venetian and *façon de Venise* goblets were made by manipulating rods and cylinders of clear or coloured glass over an open flame or "lamp".

FORMS & STYLES

Hot molten glass can be manipulated into a vast array of shapes and patterns using the main glass-forming methods of free-blowing, mould-blowing and press-moulding. Designs, even of practical glass tableware such as drinking glasses and decanters, have changed considerably over the centuries. A good knowledge of styles and decoration, as well as forming methods, used in certain periods will certainly help the budding collector in dating and authenticating glass.

The earliest glass objects – including bottles and flasks made in ancient Egypt – were generally small, heavy and irregular in shape, owing to the fact that the core-forming method used (see p.36) was impractical for large objects, since the core of sand and clay had to be laboriously dug out. The invention of free-blowing and mould-blowing by the ancient Romans enabled the production of larger vessels, few of which have, however, survived today. It was not until the development in the mid-15thC of *cristallo* – a refined, colourless type of soda glass with a long working life – that fanciful decoration, such as the serpent-shaped stems found on Venetian and *façon de Venise* drinking goblets, was widely used. Some decorative techniques, such as cutting, only became possible after the invention of heavy and brilliant lead glass in England in the 17thC as the soda and potash glass used before this period was too brittle.

Until the introduction of mechanical press-moulding in the early 19thC, which enabled inexpensive, high-volume reproductions of cut glass and other wares, glass was considered a luxury material. Early forms, such as 15th and 16thC Venetian tazzas, thus derived their shapes and decorations from silverware rather than from pottery, which was used for everyday domesticware. In turn, later glassmakers, including those manufacturing lead glass in England, were inspired by early Venetian styles. This influence is seen, for example, on the opaque and coloured twist stems of 18thC English drinking glasses.

Glass from the 18thC and 19thC is more commonly found today than that of earlier centuries. Eighteenth-century styles of lead-glass drinking glasses and decanters are generally much simpler and plainer than later ones. Early 18thC English drinking glasses had small bowls – mainly because the wine and spirits drunk at the time had a much higher alcohol content than those of today. The decoration, such as air and opaque twists and faceting, focused on the stem, which often had a knop or decorative bulbous form made by compressing the hot glass rod of the stem during manufacture. Decanters of the same period are either plain or with restrained engraving, and with matching stoppers. Heavy cutting, another speciality of Irish and English glassmakers, is characteristic of the early 19thC and is found in a wide variety of patterns, according to the type of cutting wheel: flat, curved or V-shaped. Some of the most common patterns are shown on the page opposite.

Developments in both chemical and glass technology during the Industrial Revolution enabled a much broader range of glassware to be produced, which, together with demand for reasonably priced sets of matching tableware, resulted in the emergence in the early 19thC of new types of glassware, such as butter dishes, jugs, wine-glass coolers and finger bowls. Bohemian and, later, American craftsmen were the leading exponents of coloured glass, of which many varieties were patented during this period, while acid-etching was used as an inexpensive alternative to engraving. Many pressed-glass items reproduced the cut-glass styles, but a vast array of moulding patterns, often with inventive names, was developed by American manufacturers in the later 19thC and early 20thC. Art Deco designers of the 1920s and 1930s led the trend towards geometric and angular forms, often enamelled in brightly coloured abstract patterns. In contrast, the reforming designers of the Art Nouveau and, after World War II, the studio-glass movements explored the malleable and ductile qualities inherent in molten glass in sculptural, fluid and organic forms.

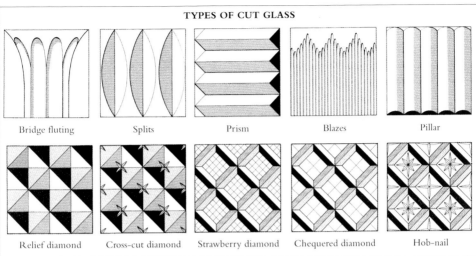

TYPES OF CUT GLASS

Bridge fluting   Splits   Prism   Blazes   Pillar

Relief diamond   Cross-cut diamond   Strawberry diamond   Chequered diamond   Hob-nail

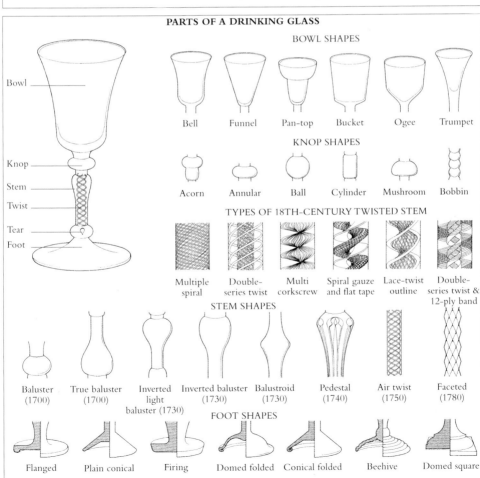

PARTS OF A DRINKING GLASS

Bowl

Knop

Stem

Twist

Tear

Foot

BOWL SHAPES

Bell   Funnel   Pan-top   Bucket   Ogee   Trumpet

KNOP SHAPES

Acorn   Annular   Ball   Cylinder   Mushroom   Bobbin

TYPES OF 18TH-CENTURY TWISTED STEM

Multiple spiral   Double-series twist   Multi corkscrew   Spiral gauze and flat tape   Lace-twist outline   Double-series twist & 12-ply band

STEM SHAPES

Baluster (1700)   True baluster (1700)   Inverted light baluster (1730)   Inverted baluster (1730)   Balustroid (1730)   Pedestal (1740)   Air twist (1750)   Faceted (1780)

FOOT SHAPES

Flanged   Plain conical   Firing   Domed folded   Conical folded   Beehive   Domed square

COPIES, FAKES & ALTERATIONS

Glass has been less widely faked than more conventionally valuable antiques. However, its popularity means that there are many copies or reproductions, especially of styles such as Regency cut glass. While most reproductions and imitations were not originally made to deceive, some, made in the late 19thC or early 20thC, are now considered antiques in their own right. Often subjected to natural wear and tear over several decades, they can sometimes be passed off as earlier pieces. Items with vulnerable points, such as handles on jugs, may have been altered or restored to make a piece usable and/or saleable. Restoration and alterations are acceptable for rare pieces but on more common pieces may detract from the value and even render the item worthless.

FAKES

Fortunately for the new collector, only a few notable types of glass have been made as counterfeit pieces, but with increasing interest in glass it is likely that forgeries in many other areas will become apparent. You should make yourself familiar with authentic pieces so you will be able confidently to identify the correct colour, weight, texture and condition.

Ancient Roman glass has been faked since the late 19thC. It is still relatively inexpensive, so you can afford to avoid pieces if you have suspicions. Original pieces, such as small bottles and flasks, should feel extremely light in weight, while modern pieces are often much heavier. Acids can also be used to

These bottles are fake "Roman" specimens, made in the Middle East in the 1960s. Mould-blown, they are decorated with Christian symbols and erotic scenes.

reproduce the iridescence, which much Roman glass has from long burial in the ground; however, always avoid pieces with iridescence on the outside only – genuine Roman glass has a metallic lustre on the inside too.

Many fakes of 19thC French and English cameo glass have appeared in recent years. Although many of these are hand-finished, like the originals, the cutting is rarely as intricate or detailed, while the colours are brighter and more "chemical" in appearance.

Associated with forgeries of complete objects is the deliberate addition of signatures to unmarked and inferior pieces of a similar date. Art Nouveau glass, especially pieces in the Gallé and Tiffany styles, sometimes features fake signatures, as does 19thC English art glass in the styles of Thomas Webb and Sons and Stevens and Williams. Since decorated pieces are often more valuable, decoration is also added to plain items. Recent engraving on old jugs and decanters can, however, be very difficult to distinguish from contemporary work if carried out by a skilled engraver.

COPIES

Numerous revivals of historical styles and anniversaries of events in the late 19thC and early 20thC have resulted in copies of earlier styles. Of English glass, the most widely imitated, and sometimes faked, are 18thC air and opaque twist-stem drinking glasses. Early 20thC copies are brighter in colour and larger than the originals, while some unscrupulous dealers have removed modern factory marks. Regency cut glass, especially decanters, has been continually produced since the early 19thC, particularly in the 1880s and 1930s. The 1930s pieces are white in tone, and have more awkward proportions than the originals; on copies of decanters the neck rings are often moulded from the body rather than made separately. From the late 19thC acid-polishing – to increase reflectiveness – was used on cut glass; this lacks the very fine traces of wheelmarks and abrasives and has rounded rather than sharp edges to the cuts.

Made from 20thC Burmese glass, this bowl and jug are an imitation of late 19thC American and English Burmese ware. The bowl is American and the jug is most likely Venetian.

In Germany the *Historismus* movement of the 1870s led to widespread reproductions of 15th and 16thC forms, such as *Roemer* with enamelled decoration. Some very high-quality decorated pieces can be confused with the originals, but many 19thC copies have over-elaborate decoration and the enamelling is too bright. Similarly, Venetian Revival pieces can be passed off as genuine 15th or 16thC pieces, but the later versions are often made of clearer glass and are heavier in weight.

DETERMINING AUTHENTICITY

Fakes and copies can often be identified by checking standard features common to glass of different periods and styles. Colour is an important indicator of authenticity – much old glass is discoloured, owing to impurities in the glass body, but with advances in technology from the late 19thC, modern glass has greater brilliance and whiteness. Weight is another factor: lead-crystal copies of pieces manufactured in soda or potash glass (before lead glass was introduced c.1700) are generally heavier and clearer, without the small bubbles or particles found in soda glass. Antique glass is also subject to wear and tear, especially the bases of decanters and the feet of drinking glasses. A magnifying glass will reveal the random pattern of scratches that characterizes authentic wear; fake wear can be identified by parallel straight lines where

the piece has been rubbed against an abrasive surface. Be wary of scratches just above the base, as this area would not normally be worn.

A pontil mark is the rough mark left by the removal of the pontil iron in free or mould-blowing. Items made before the late 18thC always have a pontil mark, but later this was often removed. Remember, though, that contemporary handmade glass is produced by similar methods, so a pontil mark is not a guarantee of authenticity or age. Modern enamelling and gilding have a bright tone and a shinier finish than earlier examples, while on genuine antique glass they may also have worn away or rubbed off through handling.

ALTERATIONS

Passing an item under ultraviolet light will show when a piece has been glued. If the foot of a drinking glass breaks off the stem might be shortened to remove the cracked edges, and the foot reattached; such items can be difficult to spot without a good visual knowledge of glasses. Rims of bowls can be ground down to remove chips and cracks. On cut or engraved pieces such alteration can be seen, as the rim will run through the decoration whereas the decoration should end just below the rim.

The Venice & Murano Glass Company paid tribute to the ancient Roman mosaic glass of the 1stC BC and 1stC AD with this rimmed shallow white-and-blue mosaic dish (c.1876).

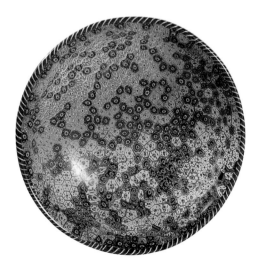

PART 4

GLASS FILE

ABOVE AN ENGLISH PILLAR–MOULDED CELERY VASE,
C.1840, £120–180/$200–290.

LEFT A SELECTION OF ANTIQUE EUROPEAN
GLASS TABLEWARE.

Drinking Glasses

Hygienic, reusable and easily cleaned, glass has been used for drinking vessels since at least ancient Roman times – mould-blown conical beakers with relief decoration from the late 1stC AD were excavated at Pompeii and Herculaneum. In the Middle Ages designs became more varied, especially on vessels made in German-speaking areas, which were often decorated with prunts ("blobs" of hot glass) and trailing. Venetian goblets from the 16thC and 17thC, with *filigrana* and *latticinio* bowls or tooled "wings" of coloured glass ornamenting the stem, are among the most sophisticated ever produced. Gradually the familiar elements of modern wine glasses – bowl, stem and foot – evolved, as seen in the great variety of English drinking glasses made in lead glass from the 18thC. Among the most immediately recognizable, and collectable, of these are the wine and ale glasses engraved with Jacobite motifs, mottoes and hymns about the Stuart descendants of King James II, considered by supporters as the rightful claimants to the English and Scottish thrones. Bowls of 18thC drinking glasses are relatively small, owing to the potency of alcoholic drinks of the time, and innovative decoration was focused mainly on the stem, with things like elegant baluster styles, air and colour-twists, and faceting. In the 19thC demand for complete table services resulted in the development of different shapes of drinking glass for red and white wine, champagne, dessert wines and liqueurs, often made in matching sets to lower manufacturing costs and make them more affordable. Greater use was made of colouring, engraving and etching to produce a variety of designs.

EARLY ENGLISH I

Before the late 17thC very few drinking glasses were produced in England; most domestic glass was imported from the Low Countries and Venice. With the development of lead glass by George Ravenscroft in 1675, distinctively English styles of drinking glass began to emerge: the earliest of these, the "baluster" style, was popular from *c.*1690 to *c.*1720. These glasses are heavy and symmetrical in form, with conical or domed folded feet and distinctive stems with one or more knops (bulbous rings), following the style of contemporary Baroque furniture.

◀ ANGLO-DUTCH GLASS
This goblet (*c.*1685) is engraved with the coat of arms of William of Orange. Diamond-point engraving was the preferred method of decoration on Anglo-Dutch glass, as the soda glass used was too fragile to be wheel-engraved. £9,500–10,000/$15,200–16,000

▶ HEAVY BALUSTER
This glass (*c.*1710) features a cushion knop with a tear over a basal ball knop and rounded funnel bowl. Baluster glasses such as this can fetch high prices, since many heavy glasses were melted down after the imposition of the 1745 Excise Tax and are consequently rare today. £2,500–3,000/$4,000–4,800

BALUSTER GLASS

This glass (c.1700) has a double knop stem. Knops on early balusters are relatively plain, but in the early 18thC more elaborate forms developed; the "egg" and "cylinder" forms are the rarest and most valuable today, followed by "mushroom" and "acorn" shapes. Virtually all baluster glasses are wine glasses and are very rarely decorated. £2,500–3,000/ $4,000–4,800

DECORATION

If, unusually, decoration such as engraved mottoes or monograms is present, it would usually have been added some time after initial manufacture.

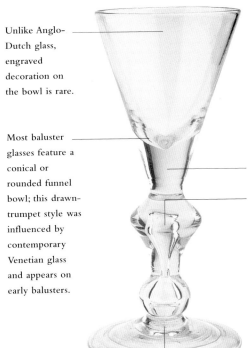

Unlike Anglo-Dutch glass, engraved decoration on the bowl is rare.

Most baluster glasses feature a conical or rounded funnel bowl; this drawn-trumpet style was influenced by contemporary Venetian glass and appears on early balusters.

The heavy solid base of the bowl is characteristic of early 18thC English baluster glasses and adds to the weight of the object.

Knops on baluster glasses from the first decade of the 18thC are often more elaborate in form.

The foot is folded to add extra strength and stability.

▶ DOUBLE KNOP STEM

This glass (c.1720) has a "true baluster" stem, with the widest part of the lower knop nearer the base, and a cushion knop. This glass features a high domed foot, but a conical foot is more common. £2,500–3,000/ $4,000–4,800

◀ MINIATURE BALUSTER

Glasses with thick-walled shallow bowls designed to hold a small quantity of alcohol were popular with publicans when drinking with their customers. Known as "illusion" glasses – as the bowl appears to be full – they were produced throughout the 18thC and 19thC. £800–1,000/$1,275–1,600

EARLY ENGLISH II

With the accession of the German Elector George of Hanover as King George I of England in 1714, new continental styles were introduced into English glass. On drinking glasses, a distinctive mould-blown stem with a hollow centre – originating in Silesia – was popular for a relatively short period (*c*.1710–30), although this style continued to be used on tazzas, candlesticks and other wares throughout the 18thC. Like baluster glasses, Silesian-stemmed glasses were very rarely decorated, and any engraved pieces will fetch a premium today. Glasses with plain stems first appeared in England *c*.1720, and were produced throughout the 18thC; the simplest style of drinking glass, they were much less expensive than earlier baluster or Silesian-stem pieces, and so were more affordable for the expanding middle-class market for domestic glass.

◀ ADAM AND EVE ENGRAVING

This goblet is one of the earliest dated English drinking glasses to have a Silesian stem. The funnel bowl is diamond-point engraved with figures of Adam and Eve and the date 1716, suggesting that it may have been a marriage gift. The inscription "God Save King George" around the shoulders of the octagonal stem is most unusual and considerably raises the value of the glass. £25,000–30,000/$40,000–48,000

▶ DRAWN-TRUMPET BOWL

This was the most common bowl shape found on 18thC plain stem glasses; the bowl and stem were made from the same gather of glass and the foot added separately. Glasses with other bowl shapes were produced in three parts. The use of a heavy folded foot dates this glass to before the 1745 Excise Act, when a tax of one penny per pound was imposed on glassmakers. £240–300/ $375–475

▲ SIX-SIDED SILESIAN STEM

The number of sides on the pedestal stem is a useful method of dating Silesian-stem glasses: the earliest have four sides, while later ones have six or eight. This glass with a double-ogee bowl and six-sided stem can be dated to *c*.1725. English versions were made from lead glass, but soda-glass versions were widely produced on the Continent. These have a light weight, dull colour and lack of ring when tapped. £450–650/$720–1,040

▶ EVERYDAY GLASS

Glasses with plain stems were
generally intended for everyday
domestic use, and thus the
quality of decoration is often
poorer than that found on more
expensive glasses with elaborate
stems: the bowl of this glass
(c.1745) features fairly crude
engraving of flowers. Fruiting
vines – relating to the use of the
glass for wine – are another
common subject on plain-stem
glasses. £200–250/$325–400

◀ CHAMPAGNE OR MEAD GLASS

This dark-green wine glass
with a cup-shaped bowl (c.1750)
would have been used for mead
or champagne; the moulding
around the bottom of the bowl
would have disguised the
sediment present in the alcohol.
While coloured English glass is
generally referred to as "Bristol"
glass, the high quality of this
piece indicates that it was
probably made in London.
£1,000–1,500/$1,600–2,400

"AMEN" GLASSES

Some of the most notable
and valuable mid-18thC
English drinking glasses
are those that are diamond-
point engraved with verses
from Jacobite hymns
ending in "Amen" (hence
the name). These glasses
were made in support of
the Old and Young
Pretenders to the thrones of
England and Scotland; only
about two dozen authentic
examples exist, and they
were widely copied in
the 19thC, although these
glasses are usually larger
than the originals.

▶ 18THC ALE GLASS

During the 18thC the size
of bowls on ale glasses was
relatively small, since the beer
of the period contained a much
higher level of alcohol than
that made today. Ale glasses
can usually be identified by the
engraved decoration of hops and
barley on the bowls, as seen
on this plain-stemmed example
of c.1770, and were widely
produced in England from
the early 18thC to the early
19thC. Such glasses are more
affordable for collectors today
than glasses with decorative
stems. £90–125/$150–200

EARLY ENGLISH III

In 1745 the British government introduced an Excise Act levying a heavy tax on glassmakers of one penny per pound of raw materials. Thereafter glassmakers attempted to reduce the overall weight of their wares – features such as folded feet and knops became much less common. The air-twist stem developed at this time as a way of making drinking glasses lighter while still maintaining a decorative element. The twist is made by making air bubbles in the gather of molten glass and then stretching and rolling it to draw them out into fine threads; such glasses were described by contemporaries as "wormed". Popular from the 1740s to the 1760s – when the opaque twist appeared – air-twist glasses often feature on the bowl diamond-point or wheel engraving of armorials, patriotic and political mottoes and slogans, commemorative themes, vine-leaf patterns and hops and barley.

WILLIAMITE GLASSES

Some rare glasses from the 1740s feature engraving commemorating the victory of William III over James II at the Battle of the Boyne in 1690. Motifs on these glasses include busts of William III and Mary II, as well as William III on horseback, with the date of the battle and/or the inscription "To the Glorious Memory". Many copies were made c.1900, so careful examination is necessary to ensure the glass is genuine.

▶ JACOBITE GLASS

This glass (c.1760) features two knops and an engraving of roses and butterflies. These are Jacobite symbols, indicating that it was made for a supporter of James Stuart, "the Old Pretender" and his son Charles Edward Stuart, "the Young Pretender". Other Jacobite emblems include forget-me-nots, thistles, daffodils, and oak trees and leaves (symbols referring to Charles II). Such glasses are highly sought after today.
£2,000– 2,500/ $3,200–4,000

◀ MIXED TWIST

As the fashion for air twists waned in the mid-18thC, and the opaque twist was introduced, some stems were made with elements of both styles, known as a mixed twist, as on the stem of this glass of c.1750. Most mixed twists feature a white opaque twist with an air twist; combined air and colour-twist stems are much rarer. Copies of such glasses were made from the mid-19thC; they are larger than the 18thC originals.
£450–550/$725–875

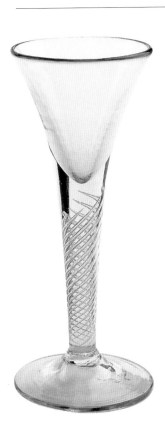

◀ MULTIPLE SPIRAL TWIST

The most common type of air twist was the multiple spiral, made from up to twelve even filaments, as seen on this glass (c.1760–65). Stems with single spirals are known as single-series air twists, while those with two different patterns of spiral, such as a "corkscrew" and a "cable", are called double-series air twists. Such glasses would have been made for everyday use in a wealthy household. £325–375/ $525–600

▶ POLITICAL ENGRAVING

Engraving on political themes was particularly popular in the mid-18thC: the figure hanging from a scaffold, the initials "AB" and the word "JUSTICE" on this glass (c.1757) refer to Admiral Byng, who was executed after being found guilty of dereliction of duty, but after his death became the focus of popular support. £1,500–2,000/ $2,400–3,200

FORMING THE KNOP ON AN AIR TWIST

Air-twist glasses were very rarely made with knopped stems: not only did a knop add to the weight of the glass, but also the technique used to create it – by pushing the stem gently back on itself – required extreme dexterity. This detail of the Jacobite drinking glass of c.1760 shows how the air bubbles thicken where the knop is created. In an air twist one or two bubbles may extend slightly further than the others because, despite the skill of the glassmaker, the bubbles are not all exactly the same size. In early examples the bowl and stem were made as one piece, with the twist at the top of the stem extending into the bowl; on this glass the bowl has been made separately and applied. This glass which has two knops is particularly rare and thus more valuable than a glass with a single knopped air-twist stem.

EARLY ENGLISH IV

The Excise Act of 1745 taxed only clear lead-crystal glass, so from the 1760s to the early 1780s glassmakers began to use opaque white or coloured glass as a form of decoration on the stems of glasses that would minimize the amount of tax paid. Opaque twist stems are produced by inserting rods of white or coloured glass into a gather of clear glass and pulling and twisting the stem to draw out the rods into fine threads, a method similar to drawing out the air bubbles in air-twist stems. The main difference between opaque and air twists is that the former are cut from a long rod, with the bowl and foot made separately and applied, while the latter are made individually, so that each one is unique. Few opaque twists were made after 1777, when another Excise Act raised a tax on coloured glass.

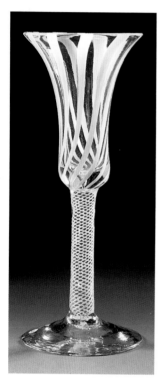

▼ TARTAN TWIST

Mixed twists with combinations of different colours and types of twist are the most sought after of 18thC English twist-stem drinking glasses. Most mixed twists feature an air twist with an opaque white twist. This highly complex "tartan twist" glass (c.1765) has an opaque corkscrew central twist edged in red and green, entwined by two outer opaque threads.
£3,000–3,500/$4,800–5,600

▲ SINGLE SERIES TWIST

Most opaque twist stems are "double-series", with one spiral within another; this single-series opaque twist glass (c.1760) is particularly rare, with the white canes of the multiple-spiral-twist stem extending to the rim of the elongated waisted bell bowl. Slight damage reduces the value. £500–700/ $800–1,125

▲ COLOURED TWIST

Generally opaque twist stems are of white glass; coloured twists are rarer, because different colours of glass have varying cooling rates, making some coloured rods more fragile and thus prone to breaking than others. This glass (c.1765) with a bell bowl and conical foot has a solid twisted blue core encased by opaque white twists; blue and yellow are much rarer coloured twists than red and green.
£2,000–3,000/$3,200–4,800

▶ **COTTON TWIST**
The stem of this glass (*c*.1760)
contains a multiple spiral opaque
twist. Glasses with opaque white
twist stems are also described
as "cotton" twists, since the very
fine white glass rods have the
appearance of cotton threads.
As with air twists, knops on
opaque twist stems are unusual
because compressing the glass
to create the bulbous ring risked
breaking the finely wrought
twist pattern inside the stem.
£400–500/$650–800

▼ **OPAQUE TWIST WITH
ROUNDED FUNNEL BOWL**
Unlike the threads of an air
twist, which become narrower at
the top of the stem, the cut end
of an opaque twist, where it was
sliced from a longer rod, will be
visible, as on this glass of *c*.1770.
The rounded funnel bowl and
foot would have been produced
separately, and a join should be
visible at both ends of the stem.
£275–325/$450–525

◀ **HIGH-QUALITY
OPAQUE TWIST STEM**
The plain bell-shaped bowl
of this glass (*c*.1770) is relatively
common on opaque twist stems
– few were engraved, unlike the
earlier air-twist stem examples.
The neatness and evenness of the
twist are a sign of high-quality
craftsmanship. Continental copies
often have uneven and poorly
formed twists as soda glass cools
more rapidly than English lead
glass. £325–375/$525–600

COMPOSITE STEM GLASSES

In the third quarter of the 18thC, glassmakers began to
produce wine glasses with stems that combined a variety
of elements, including plain, baluster and twist, in one
piece. Most of the twist elements in these so-called
"composite" stems are air twists: opaque examples
combined with knops and plain sections are much rarer.

EARLY ENGLISH V

Facet-stemmed drinking glasses represent the last attempt by 18thC British glassmakers to avoid paying the punitive taxes on glass first imposed by the 1745 Excise Act; in 1777 another Act imposed duty on coloured enamel glass, making opaque twists expensive to produce, and so the faceted stem – in which glass was cut away from the stem in decorative patterns to reduce its weight – was developed as an alternative. Popular from *c*.1780 to *c*.1810, facet-stem glasses feature three main patterns of faceting: diamond – created by cutting diagonally across the stem; hexagonal – made by cutting down and across the stem at an angle; and flat-cut – formed by slicing downwards from the bottom of the bowl to the foot. Sometimes the foot of the glass is faceted, but rarely the bowl. Instead, the bowl is often engraved with motifs of fruiting vines, chinoiserie, and egg-and-dart ornament. Until recently facet-stemmed glasses were less popular among collectors than the air and opaque twist varieties, but they have now become more valuable.

JAMES GILES

This elegant ale glass (*c*.1765) has a diamond-cut faceted stem and is gilded with a design of barley fronds. The gilding was probably undertaken in the London workshop of James Giles (1718–80), one of the most notable freelance English glass decorators working in the 1760s and early 1770s. As well as glass drinking wares, scent bottles, vases and decanters, the Giles workshop decorated porcelain from Worcester and other English factories. Designs are either gilt or enamelled, characterized by delicately painted exotic birds, chinoiserie, floral sprays and classical motifs such as husks and festoons (see tumbler on p.61). £2,000–2,500/$3,200–4,000

▶ KNOPPED FACET-STEM GLASS
Drinking glasses with this type of stem, like this example of *c*.1780–85, are rare, since forming a knop by cutting a wide stem was a time-consuming and laborious process – and also weakened the glass, so few pieces survive in good condition. Examples with more than one knop are practically unknown. The fine engraving of delicate floral garlands – a favourite motif then – also adds to the value. £400–500/$650–800

▲ TYPICAL GLASS OF THE 1790s
This style of this glass shows that, even though there was a wide variety of decorative stems throughout the 18thC, the basic shape of an English drinking glass remained unchanged, with a small rounded funnel bowl on a relatively long stem. £100–150/$160–240

EARLY 20THC COPIES

Copies of facet-stemmed glasses were produced by the firm of Stevens & Williams and the Whitefriars Glassworks in the early 20thC and are still available today. They can be distinguished from the 18thC originals by their heavier weight, thicker stems, flatter and thinner feet, and brighter colour. The laborious technique of hexagonal facet-cutting was also rarely used on such pieces.

◀ DIAMOND-CUT FACETING
Complex facet-cutting of diamond or hexagonal patterns was used on the more expensive drinking glasses, since these techniques required more dexterity and skill from the glasscutter than the simpler flat-cutting. This detail of the stem from the drinking glass opposite (top right) shows diamond-cut faceting, made by cutting diagonally across the stem. The irregular shape of the facets shows that the piece was cut by hand.

▶ HEXAGONAL CUTTING

The hexagonal style of faceted stem – created by cutting down and across the stem at an angle, as shown in this detail of the drinking glass opposite (bottom) – is less common than the diamond-cut facet variety, as it involved the removal of more glass and so created greater weakness in the stem.

◀ ALE GLASS WITH FLAT-CUT FACETS
Simple flat-cut facets were used on the more inexpensive types of drinking glass, such as this ale glass of *c*.1800, which would have been made for a tavern or for everyday home use. The flat foot is typical of facet-stemmed glasses of the late 18thC, and replaced the conical folded foot popular until *c*.1770. The top of the bowl is lightly engraved with egg-and-dart ornament, also characteristic of glasses at this time. £100–200/$160–325

PONTIL MARKS

The introduction of new mechanical grinding techniques in the late 18thC and early 19thC means that on most facet-stemmed glasses the pontil mark will be ground out.

EARLY ENGLISH VI

Made since ancient Roman times, the tumbler is the most widely produced and practical form of drinking vessel. Utilitarian versions generally consist of a plain, slightly tapering cylinder with a flat base for stability, but during the 18thC and 19thC English glassmakers produced a wide variety of decorative examples, with ornamentation ranging from fairly crude diamond-point engraving on the least expensive versions to enamelled hunting and sporting scenes, flowers, fruiting vines, landscapes and coats of arms on those made for the wealthiest clients, by glassmakers such as the Beilbys. The subject matter on most tumblers consists of humorous scenes, commemorative themes and, as tumblers were generally used for serving beer, masculine themes such as hunting. Tumblers are among the most affordable glass wares available to collectors today.

◀ RIBBED GIN TUMBLER
Lynn glass, from Norfolk, has a series of moulded horizontal ribs, the number of grooves varying from two to eight. This small tumbler of c.1780 was probably intended for gin.
£150–250/$240–400

▶ BLUE CANE RIM
In the late 18thC and early 19thC a range of practical glassware, including tumblers, jugs and ale glasses with blue cane rims, was produced in northern England.
£150–250/$240–400

WILLIAM AND MARY BEILBY

From the 1750s enamelled decoration became more common on English drinking glasses. Its best-known exponents were William Beilby (1740–1819) and his sister Mary (1749–97). William was apprenticed to an enameller, and there he began to experiment with white enamels on plain glass. In the early 1760s he started a workshop with his family in Newcastle, decorating drinking glasses, tumblers and decanters. Delicately painted white-enamel designs of landscapes, hunting scenes – such as the duck-shooting scene on this tumbler – classical ruins, or vines are typical of the Beilbys; much rarer are their armorial goblets with coloured-enamel heraldic decoration.
£4,000–6,000/$6,400–9,600

**◀ NEO-CLASSICAL
DECORATION**
This tumbler (*c.*1770) would
have been expensive when it
was made, owing to the use of
all-over gilded decoration and
white opaline glass, unusual in
English glass of the period. The
gilding was carried out by the
workshop of James Giles (1718–
80), a notable glass decorator
(see p.58), and features Neo-
classical motifs of stylized flowers,
husks, ox heads and garlands.
£2,000–3,000/$3,200–4,800

BRANDY GLASSES
While larger tumblers and
beakers would have been
used for drinking beer,
the smaller, plainer versions
may have been used in the
18thC for brandy. As they
were subject to heavy use,
comparatively few plain
pieces have survived;
decorated examples would
have been highly prized
and therefore used only
on special occasions.

▶ COMMEMORATIVE PIECE
During the 18thC and 19thC
many decorated tumblers were
produced as commemorative
pieces or presented as gifts:
this large pint-size tumbler
features a fine engraving
of lock gates and probably
commemorates the opening
of one of the many new canals
in the late 18thC and early
19thC. Such pieces can fetch
high prices today as they often
appeal to specialist collectors
with a particular historical
interest, for example in the
Industrial Revolution.
£700–800/$1,125–1,275

**◀ SUTHERLAND
TUMBLER**
This tumbler, dated 1855, is
decorated with diamond-point
engraving of various subjects,
including the royal coat of
arms. The engraver, whose style
is characterized by inaccurate
heraldic devices but high-quality
draughtsmanship, has been
identified as "Sutherland", but
no other details (not even first
name) are known. A group of
about 20–30 pieces with similar
engraved decoration has been
identified. £500–600/$800–950

LATER ENGLISH I

The fashion for heavier, more solid forms with the introduction of the Regency style from *c*.1790 to *c*.1830 brought about a dramatic change in the style of English drinking glasses at the end of the 18thC and in the early 19thC. The bowls of glasses became much wider and larger, and the stems shorter, while bowls rather than stems became the main focus of decoration. The type of drinking glass most associated with this period and style is the rummer, a large-bowled drinking goblet. The name was originally thought to have been derived from *Roemer* (a 15th–16thC type of German wine glass) but is more likely to come from the naval drink of rum and water popular at the time. While the shape of the rummer remained fairly constant through the period, decoration was varied. The most expensive examples are distinguished by heavy cutting in geometric patterns, a type of decoration linked particularly with Irish glassmakers – the relaxation of import and export duties in Ireland (then under British rule) in 1780 enabled the glass industry to flourish there, especially in Waterford, Cork and Dublin.

BRISTOL GLASS

Blue, green and amethyst glass, including drinking glasses, decanters and finger bowls, made in Britain from the late 18thC to the mid-19thC is generally described as "Bristol" glass; although Bristol was an important glassmaking centre, coloured glass was made at many other British glassworks at this period.

▶ PETAL-MOULDED RUMMER

Cutting glass is labour-intensive, so glassmakers employed mould-blowing to produce inexpensive rummers in imitation of hand-cut pieces. This petal-moulded rummer (*c*.1790–1800), so called because a flower shape is visible when you look through the glass at the bottom of the bowl, was made by blowing a gather into a shaped mould. The lightweight body and rudimentary engraving of fruit vines indicate that it was probably made for use in a tavern. £100–200/$160–325

◀ ICE CREAM GLASS OR "PENNY LICK"

This type of robust small glass with a thick-walled moulded bowl, short sturdy stem and wide flat foot is known as a "penny lick": made from the 19thC to the early 20thC for ice cream vendors to sell an old penny's worth of ice cream. A slightly larger version was called a "tuppenny lick". Such glasses are often erroneously described as illusion glasses, but can be identified by their wide bowl and thick rim. Although these are now becoming collectable, they will still fetch a fraction of the price of true illusion glasses. £20–30/$30–50

▶ **CUT-GLASS RUMMER**

This heavily-cut rummer (c.1810) would have formed part of a large and expensive table service. The combination of different types of cutting – diamond around the top of the bowl, with facets at the bottom and around the knop – is characteristic of glass made in Ireland during the Regency period. On elaborate examples such as this the foot is usually also cut. £100–150/$160–240

▶ **PLAIN WINE GLASS**

Coloured drinking glasses were popular in England from c.1790. Like this Bristol green wine glass of c.1820, they usually have a drawn-trumpet (or drawn-funnel or tulip) bowl, with a plain or knopped stem. Most coloured drinking glasses are green, with amethyst rare, and blue especially scarce and valuable. £80–100/ $130–160

◀ **REGENCY RUMMER**

A much simpler style of cutting emerged in the early 19thC; it involved cutting flat vertical slices from the glass, usually around the bottom of the bowl on drinking glasses, and was known as "broad-flute" or facet-cutting. This heavy rummer (c.1830) has a facet-cut bowl and knopped stem. £60–80/$96–130

◀ **ILLUSION GLASS**

This type of glass (c.1830) was designed to be used by either somebody proposing a series of toasts, or the landlord of an inn, who would have wanted to avoid drinking too much alcohol. The glass has a much smaller capacity than it seems as the walls of the bowl are very thick, leaving only a shallow depression for liquid at the top. These glasses were produced in England from the early 18thC but 19thC pieces are easier to find today. Earlier examples have smaller bowls and longer stems. £70–90/$120–150

LATER ENGLISH II

In the 1820s and 1830s the fashion for heavy all-over cutting in deep relief on drinking glasses began to decline, and simpler broad-flute cutting became popular. This form of decoration was much less expensive and labour-intensive than deep-relief cutting, reflecting the new wider market for reasonably priced and practical glass tableware among the increasingly affluent middle classes. This change in the social use and demand for glassware is also indicated by the popularity of the glass table service, which included various shapes and styles of drinking glass, with matching decoration, for drinks accompanying the numerous courses of elaborate Victorian dinners. Different forms of drinking glass were developed for white wine, champagne, red wine and liqueurs. At this time glasses were produced in large quantities by the major glass manufacturers in an enormous range of styles.

◀ GILDED RUMMER

19thC rummers are larger and have sturdier feet than 18thC versions. Most are plain glass, so coloured ones like this example of *c*.1800 are rare. Condition on gilded items is important as the gold often flaked off. £300–400/$475–650

▶ SIMPLY CUT RUMMER

This simply cut early 19thC rummer reflects that era's fashion for lighter styles. With the popularity of matching table services, such rummers can sometimes be found in large sets. £80–100/$130–160

VENETIAN STYLE

These champagne glasses were part of a set made for the Great Exhibition in 1851 by George Bacchus and Sons of Birmingham (est. 1840), one of the major 19thC English glass manufacturers. The glasses were illustrated in the special edition of a London magazine, the *Art Journal*, dedicated to the exhibition. Like much 19thC glassware, the design is inspired by historical sources, in this case 15th and 16th Venetian glass, which inspired the elaborate curling colour-twist stem. The high-quality engraving adds to the value. £5,000–8,000/$8,000–12,800 each

STYLES OF DRINKING GLASS

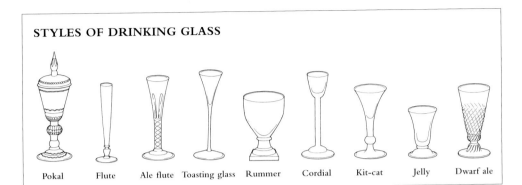

Pokal   Flute   Ale flute   Toasting glass   Rummer   Cordial   Kit-cat   Jelly   Dwarf ale

◀ ROSE PATTERN
Engraving became
the most fashionable
type of decoration
from the 1850s. While
pieces like this 1860s
goblet, decorated with
roses and signed by a
leading engraver, are
extremely rare and
valuable, most engraved
drinking glasses are
unsigned and quite
modestly priced in
today's market.
£200–300/$325–475

▶ ACID-ETCHING
The bowl of this
goblet (c.1880),
with a typically late
Victorian rounded
bowl and thin stem,
has been decorated
with an acid-etched
design. Thousands of
drinking glasses like
this were produced
from the 1830s as an
inexpensive substitute
for the more laborious
hand engraving.
£65–90/$100–150

**▶ VICTORIAN
FAVOURITE**
Drinking glasses with
coloured bowls and
clear stems were in
common use in the
last half of the 19thC.
Green and cranberry
are seen most, while
amethyst, as in this glass
of c.1880, yellow and
blue are rarer. Such
glasses were probably
made for white wines.
£80–100/$130–160

THE GREAT EXHIBITION
Held in Hyde Park, London, in
1851, this was the first major
international exhibition and gave
manufacturers around the world
a chance to show their products.
Over 150 glassmaking firms
exhibited, and the centrepiece was
a 8m/26ft-tall cut-glass fountain.

LATER ENGLISH III

In 1845 the punitive Excise Tax on glass was repealed; this gave British glass manufacturers greater opportunities to experiment with new techniques and innovative designs. High-quality cased and flashed coloured glass in the Bohemian style, for example, was produced by the leading manufacturers George Bacchus and W.H., B. & J. Richardson, both of Birmingham, J.F. Christy of London, and Stevens & Williams of Stourbridge, one of the main English glassmaking centres. The new fashion for drinking glasses which combined coloured bowls with clear stems replaced the earlier "Bristol" glass examples, which were made entirely in one colour. Engraved and etched Victorian drinking glasses are particularly representative of the new fashion for lighter decoration, replacing the much heavier and more solid styles that were popular in the early 19thC.

◀ BRISTOL GREEN
This green wine glass (c.1850) is a fairly late example of Bristol glass. Green glass was popular in the Victorian era, and was often used for serving the German wines fashionable at that time. The rounded bowl, appropriately engraved with vines, is characteristic of later 19thC Bristol glass.
£80–120/$130–200

▶ GREEK-KEY PATTERN
Wine glasses with cranberry-glass bowls and clear stems were produced by the thousand during the 19thC. This good-quality glass is engraved with a Greek-key pattern, indicating that it dates from about 1870 when there was a revival of interest in ancient Greek art.
£25–50/$40–80

▶ PRESENTATION PIECE
This goblet is engraved with the arms of the Worshipful Company of Glass Sellers of London, and dated 19 December 1878. Part of a set, it was presented to the incoming master of the guild in that year. Glass with a specific provenance, such as this, can become particularly collectable and valuable.
£350–450/$560–725

BOHEMIAN ENGRAVERS

With the fashion for high-quality engraved tableware during the mid-19thC, a number of talented Bohemian master engravers came to work for English glass manufacturers. Among the leading exponents were Paul Oppitz, who worked for W.T. Copeland in London and Frederick Kny and William Fritsche, who were employed by Thomas Webb of Stourbridge and specialized in rock-crystal engraving.

◀ FERN DESIGN

Drinking glasses with simple engraved patterns of ferns are more widely available and more reasonably priced today than more elaborately engraved or cased glasses. This example (1880–1900) was probably made as a durable but attractive tavern or hotel glass. The engraving is very sketchy and less detailed than on more expensive pieces. £50–80/$80–130

▶ GIFT SET

An elegant engraved goblet such as this would have formed part of a set of a jug and two goblets, often made as wedding gifts. The spreading foot is distinctive of drinking glasses of the 1870s. The most common themes for engravers at this time included buildings, flowers, coats of arms, fruiting vines and geometric patterns. £200–300/ $325–475

CASED GLASS

Inspired by contemporary French and Bohemian glass, English glass manufacturers began to produce sophisticated cased-glass wares, including vases and goblets, from the late 1840s. Cased glass in good condition is rare as the technique of successfully fusing glasses of different colours, which cooled at different rates, was extremely difficult to accomplish. This early 20thC hock glass by Joshua Hodgetts was made for Stevens & Williams. £1,500–2,000/ $2,400–3,200

The technique of rock-crystal engraving, characterized by deeper cutting and polished edges, is found on luxury glassware made by Stevens & Williams from the 1880s.

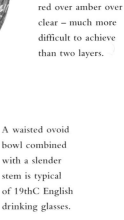

The body is made of three layers of coloured glass – red over amber over clear – much more difficult to achieve than two layers.

A waisted ovoid bowl combined with a slender stem is typical of 19thC English drinking glasses.

The star-cutting on the clear glass base is a sign of good quality.

EARLY GERMAN

Glass has been made continuously in the Rhine district since the days of the Roman Empire, and the tradition spread to central Europe during the Middle Ages. Glassmaking centres were established in the wooded forests and mountainous regions dividing Bohemia from Bavaria, Saxony and Silesia. These areas had easy access to the necessary raw materials, such as wood for fuel and minerals for the manufacture of the glass itself. Early German glass should not be confused with the high-quality glass produced in southern Germany or Bohemia. The early glass is of a type known as *Waldglas* or "forest glass", and is coloured in various shades of pale green with occasional touches of clear or dark blue. The shapes and types of these early German glass vessels are fairly primitive but nonetheless distinctive. Popular forms, such as the *Roemer*, have even survived to the present day. But by the 14thC the German glassmaking industry had really begun to develop.

◀ GREEN-TINTED *ROEMER*
The popular German drinking glass known as a *Roemer* usually has a spherical bowl, a wide, hollow stem decorated with prunts, a flared foot and perhaps a domed cover. The wide stem of this early 17thC green-tinted example is typically decorated with rows of prunts, which gave the drinker a secure grip. *Roemer* can be seen in many contemporary paintings that depict scenes of peasant life as well as in views of high society.
£12,000–15,000/$19,200–24,000

▶ 17THC *ROEMER*
The most recognizable shape of German glass used for drinking white wine, the *Roemer*, has been produced for at least 500 years. This example (*c.*1650) is unusually large but is in the typical shape, and the fat stem is decorated with raspberry-shaped prunts. Occasionally the prunts take the form of lion-head masks, and on later *Roemer* the applied prunts were drawn out into points or loops.
£6,500–9,000/$10,400–14,400

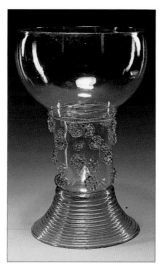

▲ ENAMELLED GLASS
The *Humpen* was one of the most distinctive items of enamelled glassware produced in 17thC Germany. This one is painted: a putto holds a skull and an hourglass within a shield. The crests and the date, 1656, may indicate that it was made to commemorate a special event.
£8,500–10,000/$13,600–16,000

► ENGRAVED TANKARD

This tankard was made in Nuremberg in *c*.1700. It has been engraved with four oval panels, each of which encloses an image of a saint, flanked by vases of flowers. The tankard was probably intended as a gift to a leading churchman. Nuremberg was a significant centre for glassware decoration from the 16thC onwards, specializing in enamelling in *Schwarzlot* and shallow wheel engraving. Many of the most accomplished glass cutters had originally practised their art engraving rock crystal and gemstones. £5,750–7,000/$9,200–11,200

WALDGLAS

From the Middle Ages the forest glasshouses of Germany made a naturally green-coloured glass known as *Waldglas*. The sand they used contained iron, which produced the green colour. Thick and robust, *Waldglas* was mould-blown in large, simple forms and decorated with designs ranging from the Biblical and mythological to scenes of daily life.

◄ ENAMELLED HUMPEN

Humpen usually belonged to important people and so were often decorated with elaborate and colourful enamelling featuring armorial bearings, figures and animals or local scenes. This fine example (dated 1719) has been painted with an Ochsenkopf Mountain scene. Early *Humpen* are rare. £5,500–8,000/$8,800–12,800

◄ RARE ENGRAVED GOBLET

This goblet (*c*.1750) is gilded and engraved with a London scene taken from a contemporary print, indicating that it was made for the wider export market. Made at the glassworks established at Potsdam in 1679 by Friedrich Wilhelm of Brandenburg, the glass exhibits some crizzling, possibly an early attempt at producing lead-crystal glass. Potsdam was famed for decorated glass, but early German glasses engraved with city views are rare. £4,000–6,000/$6,400–9,600

LATER GERMAN

Although later German drinking glasses tend to follow earlier, established forms, they also reflect a variety of recent technical advances that had been made and, owing to this, are usually made of new materials. The most important innovation of this period was the spa glass, a heavy beaker or footed tumbler that was engraved with views of a spa town. This glass was typically purchased as a souvenir by visitors seeking to "take the waters" at these popular resorts. Traditional vessels, such as *Roemer* and *Humpen*, continued to be produced, although they were frequently painted with spurious dates and crests. The union of the individual German states into one country in the late 19thC encouraged a desire to reinvent German history. This trend gave birth to the highly popular *Historismus* glassware, made in large quantities. It is often actually quite difficult to distinguish the quality examples from older originals. The new fashion for coloured and enamelled glass eventually led to a decline in the glass cutting industry.

◄ **ENGRAVED GOBLET**
This goblet (*c.*1840) is a typical example of a drinking glass imitating an earlier style. The awkward shape and harsh red colour, which is made by adding oxide of gold, iron or copper to the batch, really obscure the fine engraving of a castle. This glass was most likely made and decorated in one of the many large Rhenish glasshouses.
£90–120/$150–190

▶ **OVERLAY GLASS**
The combined labours of many skilled glassworkers created extraordinary examples of overlay glass. This goblet (*c.*1860) has been engraved with panels featuring vignettes of the forest and hunting scenes. The clear glass has been mottled, or "flecked", with red opaque glass pieces of various shapes and sizes scattered at random, then cut and engraved to highlight the relief design.
£250–500/$400–800

▲ **OVERLAID SPA GLASS**
The bowl of this robust goblet (*c.*1840) contains a panel flashed in yellow and engraved with a dedication and the name of a spa town. Spa glasses like this one were customized and made to order for visitors who had gone to a resort to take the waters. Glass engravers set up workshops in most resort towns.
£225–300/$360–475

HISTORISMUS GLASS

This beaker (c.1880) is an example of a *Historismus* glass, and was probably sold as a souvenir. Although the shape of the beaker is meant to give the impression of old glass, the colour and form did not exist before the 19thC. *Historismus* vessels can be identified by the elaborate decoration in garish enamels and false dates and crests. £120–180/$190–290

▶ HECKERT GLASS

The glass of this early 20thC goblet (c.1900) is of poor quality. However, it bears the signature of Fritz Heckert, who was a very accomplished freelance enameller and gilder. Heckert's signature adds considerably to the value of the piece. Originally from Bohemia, Heckert established a glass-decorating works in 1866 and a glass factory in 1889. He specialized in a wide variety of enamelled *Humpen*, copying woodcuts and engravings. Heckert is also known for making netted glassware and the netted-glass vessels blown into wire mesh called *Drahtlas*. £140–200/$225–325

OVERLAY

The process known as overlay involves a layer of glass being superimposed over a glass vessel. This is done by dipping the vessel into coloured molten glass, then in ground to produce a pattern. The process was popular in Bohemia during the Biedermeier period, and in England during the 19thC, and was used in France by Emile Gallé.

◀ 19THC ENGRAVED *ROEMER*

This high-quality *Roemer*, dating from c.1890, incorporates an early shape and has been enamelled by the Viennese glasshouse J. & L. Lobmeyr. The decoration of Lobmeyr's glass embraced engraved and enamelled vessels in Islamic and Oriental taste, fashionable Neo-Renaissance styles, and designs from contemporary artists and architects. £150–200/$240–320

DUTCH 18THC

Quality glass has been made in The Netherlands for several hundred years. The Dutch were a nation of traders, and their glass tends to reflect a variety of imported styles, which they often improved upon. By the late 17thC the powerful glassmaking influence of Venice had begun to wane. English glass began to be imported into The Netherlands in the early years of the 18thC, and Dutch glass produced from this period largely emulates popular English styles, having knopped glasses and air-twist and enamel-twist designs. But while The Netherland's glassmakers did not excel in the design of glass itself, they were masters at engraving it. The early method of diamond-point engraving was supplanted at the end of the 17thC by wheel-engraving, which was fashionable in the glass centres of Bohemia and Silesia. By the mid-18thC the technique of stippling with the diamond point was adopted; this rendered variations of light and shade with great delicacy. Glasses were engraved with a host of popular subjects to celebrate marriages, friendship, battles, leisure pursuits and politics.

▼ DIAMOND-POINT ENGRAVED GOBLET

This fine baluster-shaped goblet (c.1680) has been influenced by the styles of contemporary English lead glass. The deep funnel bowl has an inscription diamond-point engraved above a continuously fruiting vine, and the foot has also been engraved with a band of leaves and flowers. In The Netherlands the art of diamond-point engraving was very advanced, and it developed more swiftly there than it did in other glassmaking countries. This technique, for example, is rarely found on glasses engraved in England before the 18thC. £6,000–9,000/$9,600–14,400

▶ NEWCASTLE GLASS GOBLET

The bowl of this "Newcastle light baluster" goblet (c.1745) is engraved with a three-masted ship flying a pennant inscribed with the monogram of the Dutch East India Company. Such glasses were often made to celebrate a merchant voyage. £8,000–10,000/$12,800–16,000

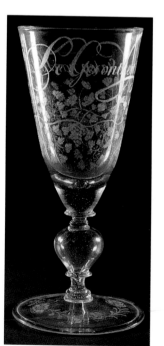

"NEWCASTLE" GLASS

Throughout the 18thC the influential lead glass known as "Newcastle" glass was the popular choice of Dutch engravers. (It is now thought to have been made in The Netherlands, not England.) This glass was preferred because it was a bright and lustrous material that displayed engraved motifs to best advantage and, stylistically, was delicately fashioned and of elegant form.

▶ WHEEL-ENGRAVED GLASS

Because of its superior refractive power and soft nature, well-suited for work on the wheel, English lead crystal was often favoured by Dutch engravers. Glasses such as this fine armorial goblet (*c*.1760) may have been made in England and engraved in The Netherlands, although it is now thought possible that they are all Dutch. This example, with its coroneted shield cartouche surrounding a rampant lion crest, was engraved by Jacob Sang, one of the most highly accomplished 18thC Dutch wheel-engravers.
£5,000–7,500/$8,000–12,000

▶ ENGRAVED BEAKER

This beaker (*c*.1760) has been engraved with a design composed of the seven states, or Stads, of The Netherlands. Made to demonstrate the importance of national unity, beakers like the one shown here were popular vehicles for expressing the political sentiments of the day. The heavy shape is typical of mid-German glass of the same period.
£80–160/$130–260

▶ RED AND WHITE TWIST WINE GLASS

Glasses with stems of coloured spirals have long been admired, and remain highly popular among collectors. Although designed in the English style, this red and white twist wine glass (*c*.1780) has been made of soda glass, which was common in England before lead glass was developed in 1676. Because soda glass cools quickly, the twist on the stem of this example has not been rendered with the sharpness of versions produced in English lead crystal.
£220–270/$350–430

EARLY BOHEMIAN

An important glassmaking centre from the 15thC, Bohemia, the area adjoining Bavaria and Silesia, now part of the Czech Republic, pioneered the formula for a colourless, easy-to-cut glass, which incorporated lime derived from chalk or limestone. By the late 16thC the use of this lime glass, which facilitated the perfection of wheel-engraving, had spread to other glass centres on the Continent. The making of engraved glass has traditionally been a Bohemian speciality, with vessels sculpturally cut in relief or engraved in intaglio, or a richly wrought combination of both. Popular subjects for engraving on early Bohemian glass include coats of arms, portraits of princes, the ages of man, the seasons, classical mythology and courtly life. From the end of the 17thC Bohemian salesmen carried their product throughout the world. The glassware was decorated to order, as the salesmen were also skilled engravers who filled the demand for this coveted commodity on the spot.

◀ HALL-IN-TYROL GLASS
Hall-in-Tyrol, an important centre, was founded in 1534 and prospered until 1602, producing ewers and goblets in colourless, blue or green glass, like this *façon de Venise* example, decorated with a beechnut pattern. £20,000–25,000/$32,000–40,000

▶ PUZZLE GOBLET
This amusing green-tinted glass is a "puzzle goblet" (or *Scherzgefas*) – a type of glass that was popular in 17thC Germany. Here the funnel bowl supports the detachable figure of a stag. This unusual form of drinking glass was designed to make drinking difficult, and to amuse companions. These joke glasses came in a variety of frivolous shapes, including shoes, boots and various animals. £6,000–9,000/$9,600–14,400

▶ FACETED GLASS
The distinctive dark blue of this faceted goblet (*c.*1750) was first produced in Bohemia in the 16thC. The vivid colour, achieved by adding cobalt oxide to the batch, was first used in Roman times. It was reintroduced by Venetian glassmakers in the 17thC, and was adopted at glassmaking centres throughout Europe. £2,500–3,500/$4,000–5,600

ZWISCHENGOLDGLAS
In this process, developed in the early 18thC, gold or silver leaf was applied to the outer surface of a drinking glass, then delicately engraved with hunting scenes or armorial crests and protected by a larger glass sleeve over the top.

JOHANN JOSEF MILDNER

The Austrian Johann Josef Mildner's (1763–1808) glassware most famously features medallion panels and borders decorated on the inner side in gold leaf and red lacquer, inserted into cut-out spaces.

▶ MILDNER TANKARD

This covered tankard (c.1799) was made by the Austrian glassmaker Johann Josef Mildner, who in 1787 revived and elaborated the method of making sandwich gold glass, or *Zwischengoldglas*. He is also widely celebrated for perfecting *Medaillonbecher*. This tankard is a fine example of his work as it features the ruby-lacquered ground and diamond-point engraving that were the hallmarks of his decorative style. £14,000–17,000/ $22,400–27,000

▲ OPAQUE TWIST

The technique of decorating the stems of drinking glasses by twisting a rod of opaque white or coloured glass originated in Rome and Venice. Opaque white glass was created by the addition of tin oxide to the batch. The stem of this 18thC goblet (c.1770), called a "cotton twist", features a "double-series" of opaque twist, where one spiral is contained within another. £250–500/$400–800

SCHWARZLOT

This late 17thC goblet, with its later decoration (c.1735), incorporates *Schwarzlot*, a technique of black-lead enamelling that emulates engraving. Used principally by German *Hausmaler* from the second half of the 17thC until the 1750s, mostly on porcelain, *Schwarzlot* was introduced on glass at Nuremberg and used by Bohemian glassmakers in the early 18thC. Designs consisted mainly of battle scenes, mythological subjects, landscapes and, as shown here, hunting scenes. Iron red and gilding were sometimes added, and fine details etched with a needle. Reproduction *Schwarzlot* glassware became popular in the 19thC. £3,800–4,500/$6,075–7,200

LATER BOHEMIAN I

Bohemian glass produced during the early 19thC was technically some of the best ever made. There was an enormous amount of experimentation in colours and types of glass as well as great skill in the decoration during this period. Much of the glass was never intended to be used, but was made as cabinet pieces designed to show off the wealth and taste of the owner. During the Biedermeier period in the mid-19thC, when coal supplanted wood as fuel owing to the reduced supply of timber, many glassmaking factories were established throughout Bohemia. The emerging middle class preferred a lighter, more intimate style, in sharp contrast to the heavy Empire taste, and the Biedermeier glassmakers answered this demand with the use of finely detailed decoration and subtle new colours. Towards the middle of the century, skill in design and decoration overtook taste to some extent, and a number of the items became over elaborate, although even today these pieces have their admirers and collectors.

▶ **ENAMELLED BEAKER**
This rare Viennese beaker (dated 1806) has been enamelled with nine tarot cards. The high quality of the decoration rivals the finest work found on porcelain produced in Vienna at this time. The cards may have had political significance. The styles of enamelled glass produced after 1800 are many and varied. Enamelled wares from the early 19thC feature landscapes, floral designs and portraits. £6,000–6,500/$9,600–10,400

◀ **STAINING**
This robust faceted goblet (*c*.1850) was decorated with yellow staining and engraved with a scene of stags and hinds. Friedrich Egermann invented this inexpensive way of colouring glass; it was used on mass-produced 19thC wares. The method involved painting an object with a coloured stain, then firing it at a low temperature to produce the effect of flashing. £1,500–2,500/$2,400–4,000

▶ **RUBY-STAINED GOBLET**
Monumental glassware, such as this large ruby-stained lidded goblet and cover (*c*.1860), was generally designed for display purposes. The engraving is often of very high quality, but the subjects tend to be hunting scenes, as seen on this finely engraved example with its two running stags. £1,850–2,000/$2,960–3,200

◀ RUBY-FLASHED GOBLET

The rounded funnel bowl of this Bohemian ruby-flashed covered goblet (mid-19thC) has been engraved with a charming wooded landscape scene of two stags flanking a hind that have been suddenly surprised by three noisy ducks. Flashing, if it incorporated a contrasting colour, could be cut through to produce a pattern that is not unlike the cameo glass that was made by the Romans. This technique was especially popular with the Bohemian glassmakers of the Biedermeier period. £1,000–1,250/$1,600–2,000

▶ PEWTER-MOUNTED ROEMER

This miniature *Roemer* (*c.*1880) has been made of ruby glass, with a pewter foot. Tankards and jugs were commonly made with pewter lids, but glasses like this unusual example, which was used for drinking schnapps, are rarely found mounted with pewter. £120–150/$190–250

▶ YELLOW GLASS ROEMER

Decorated with a finely engraved Bacchus, the god of wine, surrounded by vine leaves, this yellow glass *Roemer* (*c.*1860) would have been made as part of a larger wine set comprising a jug or decanter and six, eight or even more wine glasses (possibly of differing colours). The yellow colour was created by adding uranium to the batch, a technique developed by the Bohemian glassmaker Josef Riedel in the 1830s. The engraving on this particular piece is unusually good. £150–250/$240–400

RUBY GLASS

At the end of the 17thC a deep pink glass was invented by Johann Kunckel, a director and chemist at the Potsdam Glasshouse. The colour was produced by adding gold chloride to the batch. Known as "Kunckel red", *Rubinglas* or *Goldrubinglas*, it was also made at Nuremberg and other glasshouses in south Germany. Gold ruby glass was usually considered a luxury product.

LATER BOHEMIAN II

By the early 20thC, glassware being made in Bohemia had developed into an interesting and highly innovative product, surpassing the fine quality but rather repetitive, lacklustre style of the early 19thC. Spearheaded by the *façon de Venise* factory of J. & L. Lobmeyr, many new styles were produced, beginning with the Baroque revival and spanning the influential periods of Art Nouveau (or *Jugendstil*) to Art Deco. Many glasshouses were opened in Bohemia between 1900 and the 1920s. Among the most prominent

and successful of these factories were those at Haida and Karlsbad, where the glassmaker Ludwig Moser (1833–1916) made glass portraits in the style of Dominik Biemann, who had worked during the first half of the 19thC. Traditional Bohemian designs continued to be produced into the 20thC, but the copies hardly matched the elegant proportions of the originals, and the workmanship rarely equalled the superb quality of cutting and engraving found in early Bohemian glassware.

▶ BLUE-STAINED GOBLET

This blue-stained goblet (*c.*1850) reflects the heavy style typical of the 19thC. However, it has been engraved with a scene of a young boy wearing Scottish highland dress, thus reflecting the international character of the glass trade by the mid-19thC. The goblet may have been made by the distinguished 19thC engraver Karl Pfohl. £7,000–8,500/ $11,200–13,600

▶ HOCK GLASS

This drinking glass is an example of Theresienthal glass, which originated in the 19thC. It is a hock glass – intended to hold any white wine – and these were often made as part of a set. The globular bowls are variously coloured and sometimes have gilded decoration. The quality does vary. £400–600/$650–950

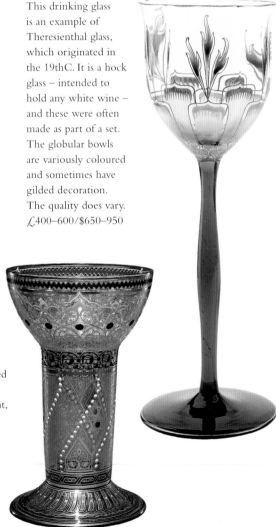

▶ EXOTIC BEAKER

Designed and signed by Franz Schmoranz for the celebrated firm of J. & L. Lobmeyr, this exotic beaker (*c.*1900) has been decorated with rich gilding and thick blue-and-white enamelling in a pattern of dense scrolling arabesque foliage and geometric ornament. It was made for the Islamic market. While English glass was aimed at Europe, the USA and, to a certain extent, India, Bohemia had created a profitable business exporting to the Ottoman Empire. £6,000–8,000/ $9,600–12,800

◀ **ENAMELLED HOCK GLASS**
This hock glass (*c.*1900) is
a product of the celebrated
glasshouse Theresienthaler
Kristallglasfabrik. This fine
example has been enamelled
with a leaf design, a decorative
motif favoured during the
Jugendstil (the German name
for the Art Nouveau

movement). Although they
were never meant to be
included in larger glassware
services, the hock glasses,
liqueur glasses, finger bowls
and decanters made in this
particular style captured
popular imagination for a
brief time from 1904.
£120–150/$190–$240

▶ **ART NOUVEAU GLASS**
A product of the Bohemian
glassmaking centre of Novy
Sust, this lovely wine glass
(*c.*1900) has been deeply carved
with the image of an iris, a
favourite Art Nouveau motif.
Whereas earlier decoration had
paid scant notice to the shape
of the body to which it was
applied, this glass has been
conceived as and made in the
shape of a graceful flower,
testifying to the unity of design
and decoration that was a
hallmark of the Art Nouveau
style. The glass invites the
drinker to sip the scented
liqueur while holding the
delicate flower-like stem.
£250–300/$400–475

**THERESIENTHAL
GLASS**
The Theresienthaler
Kristallglassfabrik was
a Bavarian glasshouse
founded in 1836 by
Prague natives Frans and
Wilhelm Steigerwald. The
factory was directed by
the Poschinger family
from 1861. It achieved
fame for its engraved,
cased and flashed glass,
as well as for drinking
glasses that mirrored
earlier German and
Venetian fashions. In the
earlier 20thC it produced
decorative iridescent glass
in the Tiffany style as
well as tablewares based
on the ideas of designer
Hans Christiansen.

◀ **ART DECO TUMBLER**
At the forefront of Art Deco
design, this tumbler (*c.*1910),
made in an 18thC style, was
produced by the distinguished
firm of J. & L. Lobmeyr and
engraved by the glassmaker
Michael Powolny with an
allegorical scene. The firm was
known for *hochschitt* and *tiefschnitt*,
as well as for enamelled and
iridescent ware. £2,500–3,000/
$4,000–4,800 (for a set of four)

FRENCH

From the 12thC France has boasted a thriving industry in the manufacture of fine stained glass, mirrors and plate glass, but there existed no parallel tradition in the production of quality table glass. Until the end of the 18thC, France lagged far behind the rest of Europe, concentrating only on simple wares made of greenish forest glass (*verre de fougère*). Although glassworks had been established throughout France, and there were important centres at Nevers, Rouen, Orleans and Nantes, no effort was made to imitate the highly influential styles of other European glassmakers. Some distinction in creating Venetian-style glass was achieved by the glassworkers at Nevers, who had emigrated from the important glassmaking centre of L'Altare near Genoa. But it was mainly only the large factories of Baccarat, St Louis and Clichy that from the late 18thC became celebrated for fine-quality cut glass, cameo glass, engraved glass and paperweights.

◀ TUMBLER BY BACCARAT
Importing knowledge and labour from many factories in Europe in the late 18thC, St Louis and Baccarat produced superb crystal table glass, as seen in this beautifully cut Baccarat tumbler (*c.*1840).
£120–150/$190–240

▶ BISTRO GLASS
This late 19thC bistro glass is typical of the French glassware that was made for the mass market. Although this cheap glass is attractive and serviceable, a close inspection of it reveals it to be poorly made from a mediocre material.
£70–85/$115–135

CAMEO GLASS
The fashion for cameo decoration on glass spread from England to France, where factories such as Baccarat and the St Louis Glassworks produced many fine hand-carved pieces. As the demand for cameo glass grew, short cuts were introduced to relieve the labour-intensive process and produce affordable cameo glass. This goblet is an example of the collectable **faux** *wares.* £680–750/ $1,090–1,200

The bowl is decorated with a rustic scene of a country boy tending his sheep. The detail is not as fine as that found on hand-carved cameo glass.

The *faux* cameo has been created with acid applied to cut away the design: a cheap alternative to hand carving.

This goblet was made at the St Louis Glassworks (*c.*1880). It was designed as a display piece for a collector's cabinet.

Top layers of *faux* cameo are thinner than those found on true cameo glass. The definition between each of the different layers is also not as sharp, the edges of the decoration are softer, and the background appears matt and slightly rough to the touch.

**▶ HOCK GLASS
BY BACCARAT**
Beautifully made and
finely decorated, this
yellow-green hock glass
(c.1890) by Baccarat is
typical of the style
popular at the end of
the 19thC. Impressive
glassware such as this
was a stylish addition
to the well-dressed
dining table.
£200–250/$325–400

◀ STEM GLASS
This Silesian stem
glass (c.1750) exhibits
the strong stylistic
influence of glassware
made in Britain and
The Netherlands in
the 18thC. However,
its inferior quality
and crude manufacture
betray its origins as
a French product.
£150–250/$250–400

**◀ FOREST GLASS
(*VERRE DE FOUGÈRE*)**
This drinking glass,
known as forest glass,
or *verre de fougère*, dates
from the early 18thC,
and is of a type that
was made continuously
from the early 17thC
until the beginning of
the 19thC. Produced
at many small
provincial glassworks,
these unremarkable
glasses were typically
made in poor-quality
soda glass, and have
no real market value
outside France itself.
£80–120/$130–190

BACCARAT
The Baccarat
Glassworks were
established in 1764.
The most important
maker of crystal glass
in France that still
flourishes today, it
is known for its fine
stemmed tableware
of incredible thinness,
and for stressing form
over decoration.

EARLY VENETIAN

From the beginning of the 16thC, Venetian glass set the standard for glassmakers in the whole of Europe. Owing to Venice's superior trading position, its authoritarian government and guild structure, early Venetian glass (1500–1800) was widely exported, although the secrets of its production were jealously guarded. The Venetian glassmaking industry was based on the island of Murano, and the fine *cristallo* glass made there, along with coloured glass and highly prized vessels emulating precious stones, such as onyx, agate and chalcedony, was the envy of Europe. However, by the late 17thC the supremacy of the Venetian glass industry had begun to decline, largely through the extreme fragility of the glass and its increasing role as a merely decorative novelty. While the popular taste for artistically decorated glassware continued to grow, the overall demand was for a more serviceable and robust type of glass. This was much more successfully satisfied by the competitive glassworks that were situated in both England and Bohemia.

▶ **LION-MASK STEMS**
The knop of this green-tinted goblet (from the second half of the 16thC) has been decorated with lion masks and rosettes. Drinking glasses with moulded lion-mask stems were common products of both Venice and *façon de Venise* glasshouses throughout Europe. As the attribute of St Mark and the symbol of the city of Venice, the lion mask was a popular decorative motif for Venetian glassware, ornamenting hollow blown stems or moulded in relief on prunts.
£6,000–8,000/$9,600–12,800

◀ **RARE 16THC WINE GLASS**
During the 16thC, lightness and elegance of form were highly prized in glassware. This fine wine glass (*c*.1560), with applied wings and a twisted stem, is a rare prototype for much of the "tourist" glass made in Venice today. Although practically imprisoned in order to protect their precious glassmaking recipes, Venetian glassmakers nonetheless gave full range to their fertile and creative imaginations, as this rare original example demonstrates.
£8,650–10,000/$13,840–16,000

FILIGRANA
In this method, also known as *latticinio,* fine threads of opaque white glass are embedded in the clear glass, forming a network pattern. The intricate designs produced by the process include *vetri a filato* and *vetri a reticello.*

◀ CRISTALLO TAZZA

The decoration of this shallow tazza or wine glass (*c.*1600) has been applied "cold" – that is, after the vessel has been made. It is decorated with diamond-point engraving, the only technique gentle enough to be used on the very thin and delicate *cristallo* glass. The fragility and thinness of Venetian glass made wheel-cutting and engraving virtually impossible. £5,000–6,000/ $8,000–9,600

▼ ENAMELLED MUG

This squat enamelled mug (*c.*1730), decorated with a variety of vividly coloured flowers above sprigs of stylized daisies, was designed for the Turkish market. The clear ground of *cristallo* glass, developed by the Murano glassmaker Anzolo Barovier in the mid-15thC, was ideal for the brightly tinted enamelled decoration. £5,000–6,000/ $8,000–9,600

▶ FILIGREE GOBLET

Filigree glass, sometimes called lace glass, was first recorded in 1527 when the glassmaker Bernardo Serena and his brother Filippo applied for a patent to make "a glass of stripes of white and other colours". This rare Venetian covered goblet (*c.*1600), decorated in the technique of *vetri a reticello*, is a tour de force of technical virtuosity that testifies to the skills of the Murano glassmakers. The fine threads of white glass have been cut, flattened, joined together and then shaped into the goblet at extremely high temperatures. Such popular patterns were produced until the 18thC. Precise dating is hard, as glass in this style was made in other parts of Europe. £10,000–12,500/ $16,000–20,000

LATER VENETIAN

By the mid-18thC, the status of the celebrated Venetian glassmaking industry had suffered a dramatic decline. This loss of prestige was largely the result of strong competition from other glassmaking centres, most notably those in England and Bohemia. With the end of the Austrian occupation in 1866, the reputation of Venice as an important glass centre was restored as makers rediscovered the decorative techniques and intricate Venetian patterns of glass recipes from the 16thC. A key figure in this revival was Antonio Salviati, a medical doctor who brought together the most highly skilled craftsmen on Murano. Using British capital, he established the Venice and Murano Glass Company, first displaying his wares at the London International Exhibition of 1862 and enjoying further success at the 1867 exhibition in Paris. Salviati, and the entrepreneurs who followed him, produced mainly tableware, freely based on Venetian glass styles from the 16thC and 17thC, but usually more richly coloured. These purely ornamental pastiche copies of early Venetian glass proved to be enormously popular, and they influenced the glassmaking industry right across Europe.

◀ SALVIATI CUP AND SAUCER SET
This pretty cup and saucer (c.1920) have been signed by Salviati. Such a signature is an unusual feature, and therefore will add to the overall value. The cup and saucer were not made to be used but to be placed together in a cabinet as a decorative piece. The quality of Salviati glass varies, from superbly crafted vessels to crudely coloured examples. £120–150/$190–240

▼ UNUSUAL LACE DESIGN
The unusual lacy decoration on this Salviati display cup and saucer (c.1920) is achieved by using real lace fabric covered with enamel. When the enamel is fired the lace material burns away, leaving the delicate lace pattern on the surface. £180–210/$290–340

▶ SHIP GOBLET
This fanciful goblet or *aquamanile* (c.1860) was made as a table centrepiece. In the form of a ship, it is a typical example of the extravagant copies of earlier styles popular in the 19thC. Few such highly impractical pieces have survived undamaged. £2,000–2,500/$3,200–4,000

▶ FLOWER DISH

Designed in the shape of a petalled flower, this dish (c.1890), which rests on three tiny feet, has been made in the fashionable Art Nouveau style. It is decorated with an alternating pattern of dark and light stripes, a technique that recalls the elaborate striped decoration favoured on Venetian glass of the 17thC. £120–150/$190–240

◀ SALVIATI GOBLET

Made by Salviati (c.1900), this white goblet is typical of the tableware associated with later Venetian glassmakers. It is made with canes of glass, in the elaborate manner originating in the 17thC, although it has been adapted for modern, everyday use. This decorative technique remains labour intensive, even today, and vessels in this style continue to command very high prices. Salviati specialized in reproductions of antique Venetian glass, including vases, bottles, goblets and tazzas with elaborate stems. The company played a vital role in popularizing the Venetian style in Britain and the USA and throughout Europe. £500–600/$800–950

▶ TOURIST GLASSWARE

This pink dish (c.1920) is a typical example of the glassware aimed specifically at the tourist market. It is well made and elaborately decorated, which shows the technical skills of the glassmaker, but the design has little artistic merit. The tourist trade was at that time largely served by individual lamp workers, who specialized in drinking wares decorated with complex figures and intricate ornament. £400–480/$650–775

LATTIMO GLASS

By 1500 a pure white glass had been perfected by Venetian glassmakers. Known as *lattimo*, or milk glass, this style tried to emulate the highly prized porcelain of China and was used for some of the finest enamelled glassware.

AMERICAN

American drinking glasses present a wealth of choice for the glass enthusiast: as well as fine cut and engraved glasses, often inspired by European luxury tableware, a broad variety of tumblers, goblets and other drinking vessels in unusual coloured and opalescent glass was manufactured during the 19thC and early 20thC. American pieces were originally made from flint (lead) glass – a perfect medium for pressed glass – and although flint was not used from the 19thC, the name remained. However, the majority of American glasses that survive today are made from non-flint material (non-lead), providing a lighter and less brilliant finish than flint. As in Europe, matching drinking glasses formed part of a larger table service, or were produced in pairs or sets with decanters and jugs as presentation pieces or wedding gifts. Forms are also similar to styles across the Atlantic (bowls are wide and round and set on narrow stems), but the wide range of colours and decorative motifs is distinctively American.

▶ **FERNS AND LEAVES**
This champagne glass (c.1890), acid-etched with a pattern of ferns and leaves, was designed and made by the English-born Joseph Locke (1846–1936). Acid-etching was generally regarded as an inexpensive substitute for engraving, but the decoration on this piece is finely detailed and may have been finished by hand. As on the best-quality etched and engraved drinking glasses, the signature appears within the decoration – here it reads "Locke Art" and is at the bottom of the bowl.
£150–200/$240–325

JOSEPH LOCKE
Joseph Locke originally worked for the English firm of W. H., B. & J. Richardson, near Stourbridge in the Midlands. He emigrated to the USA in 1882 and began working at the New England Glass Co., where he invented a variety of techniques for colouring and etching glass, including "Amberina" glass.

◀ **"EXCELSIOR" PATTERN**
The rapid expansion in the production of pressed glass in the USA in the first half of the 19thC resulted in an endless variety of named patterns, often used by several manufacturers. This "Excelsior" pattern opalescent lead-glass tumbler (1850s–60s) has been attributed to several firms, including the Boston & Sandwich Glass Co. and the McKee Brothers of Pittsburgh. The pattern may be inspired by Gothic architectural tracery. Examples in clear glass are relatively common; coloured and opalescent pieces are much rarer. £30–95/$50–150

OPALESCENT GLASS

Opalescent glass was often used for pressed-glass wares in the USA from the 1830s onwards and was made by adding phosphate – as powdered calcined animal bones – to the batch. While the glass initially appears a milky blue, it will have a fiery red tint when held up to the light.

◀ "COLONIAL" PATTERN
The sturdy form and thick low stem of this 1850s opalescent drinking glass in the "Colonial" pattern are typical of the robust lead-glass vessels made in the 19thC. Like many US examples it may have been one of a large set with a matching decanter or jug, possibly for white wine or sherry. Always check for cracks or chips around the foot, the rim and the top of the stem, as damage can render items worthless. £125–250/$200–400

▶ "PIGS IN CORN"
This pair of pressed glass goblets, with the design on one mirroring that on the other, was probably made as a presentation set. Unlike most patterns, "Pigs in Corn" was never used on complete sets of tableware. Coloured "Pigs in Corn" drinking glasses are especially scarce. £190–325/$300–500 (each)

◀ VINE-LEAF DESIGN
Designs of scrolling vine leaves, as seen on this pressed glass "Maine" pattern goblet (c.1899), made in Pittsburgh, have always been popular on wine glasses. The simple pattern of beading between the panels was also used to create lettering on English mould-pressed glass, especially that made by Henry Greener & Co. of Sunderland. Pressed glass such as this can be identified by the smooth interior, whereas on mould-blown glass the pattern on the exterior can be discerned on the inside. £125–250/$200–400

BELGIAN & DUTCH

It took nearly 100 years for the secrets of Venetian glassmaking to escape into the wider world. By the early 17thC there was a sizeable group of emigrant Venetian glassmakers working throughout Europe, including in the Low Countries (now Belgium and The Netherlands). Antwerp was a major glassmaking centre, which attracted many of the finest Venetian workmen. At first they produced high-quality copies of popular Venetian glass, but before long a style loosely based on the Venetian style began to emerge, known as *façon de Venise* (in the Venetian manner). Vessels were often made of thin soda glass and decorated with *filigrana* or ornate embellishments such as winged glasses. The most accomplished of early *façon de Venise* pieces are often difficult to distinguish from original Venetian work.

◀ RARE CASED BEAKER

The style of this cased beaker from the south of The Netherlands (c.1600) draws on early Venetian examples. Made of tinted soda glass, it might be confused with glass produced in Venice 50 years earlier. The bright colour splashed over the surface is a clue to its origin. £14,000–17,000/$22,400–27,200

▶ WINGED GOBLET

This turquoise-blue winged goblet (c.1680) is of a type that has been attributed to Venetian glasshouses. It is now thought to come from the Low Countries as, despite the style, the colours and awkward construction indicate that it could not have been made in Venice. £12,000–14,000/$19,200–22,400

▶ SLENDER WINE FLUTE

The slender conical bowl of this serpent-stemmed wine flute (c.1680) has been engraved with a hunting scene. The flute form is a shape typically found in the Low Countries, although the wings and diamond-point engraving indicate Venetian influence. Hunting scenes were popular subjects in the 17thC. £25,000–30,000/$40,000–48,000

FAÇON DE VENISE

By the 16thC Antwerp had become the most important glassmaking centre in the Low Countries, attracting highly skilled workmen from Venice. Venetian-style glass, known as *façon de Venise*, was made in vast quantities to meet the growing demand created by local patrons, who sought to publicize their wealth and status with displays of glassware in this celebrated style. £10,000–15,000/$16,000–24,000

● The substantial shape of this *façon de Venise* goblet originated in the Low Countries.

● The decorative blob, or bulge, on the stem of the glass is a normal feature. It can be hollow or solid and in a variety of shapes, including ball, cone, button, acorn, annular, and ovoid, as in this example.

● The folded foot adds extra strength. The rim is slightly turned under to make a double layer of glass, lessening the risk of breakage.

● The calligraphic inscription on the cup-shaped bowl has been rendered in diamond-point engraving. Anna Roemers Visscher and William Jacobsz van Heemskerk perfected such decorative script in the 17thC. Often, glasses of this kind were made to celebrate a marriage or the birth of a child.

◀ **LION-MASK BEAKER**
The surface of this beaker (*c.*1650) has applied lion-mask prunts representing the Lion of St. Mark – the symbol of the city of Venice. It is likely that this beaker was made by Venetian workers who had emigrated to the Low Countries in the 17thC. £600–800/$950–1,275

WINGED GLASS

These goblets, made in 16th and 17thC Venice, were widely copied in the Low Countries. The stem was decorated with designs of applied threading in coloured glass.

▶ *FAÇON DE VENISE* **GOBLET**
This interesting, double-walled *façon de Venise* goblet with silver-foil inclusions was made towards the end of the 18thC. The shape of the goblet resembles the designs commonly found in English glass. However, the silvered decoration remains in Continental style, underlining the fact that the Low Countries were actually a melting pot of a variety of European influences. £3,000–5,000/$4,800–8,000

Decanters

In the strictest sense of the term, a decanter is a vessel used to store wines such as port and madeira that have been decanted from another vessel to remove sediment. However, it is now used much more broadly to describe any type of tall, stoppered glass vessel for storing and serving drinks.

In England dark-green seal bottles were made from the mid-17thC, but decanters in colourless lead glass first appeared at the beginning of the following century. Styles altered quite considerably over the years – early 18thC forms are tall and tapering, sometimes decorated with simple engraving of motifs such as festoons and fruiting vines, while heavily cut bulbous ovoid shapes, with shorter necks with applied moulded rings for ease of handling, are associated with the Regency period from *c.*1805 to *c.*1830. Initially decanters were provided with corks – it was not until the 1750s that glass stoppers were introduced. Like decanter shapes, these too were produced in a variety of styles throughout the 18thC and 19thC, from the faceted disc, lozenge and bull's-eye shapes to the flat-mushroom and faceted-ball ones. Decoration on the body of the decanter matching that on the stopper is a good indication that both parts were made at the same time. Coloured decanters first appeared in blue "Bristol" glass at the end of the 18thC but became more popular in the Victorian era for serving the white wines fashionable at the time. Today many collectors look for matching pairs or sets of decanters, which, if in good condition, are usually more valuable than single items.

EARLY ENGLISH I

The earliest English lead-glass decanters, made in the first two decades of the 18thC, followed the style of contemporary dark-green seal bottles and often had projecting rims at the top for corks on strings as stoppers to be attached. However, forms of decanter evolved rapidly throughout the century, gradually becoming taller and more elegant until the development of the Indian club and ovoid shapes in the 1770s and 1780s. Glass stoppers replaced the functional corks in the mid-18thC.

◀ STARS AND FACETS
Often made in pairs, this style is known as a "taper" decanter, from its shape, and was popular from the late 1760s. Taper decanters are often plain, but this example (*c.*1770) is faceted around the neck and base and on the stopper, with decorative cutting of stars around the body.
£400–500/$650–800

▶ ENGRAVED MONOGRAM
The Indian-club shape appeared in the 1770s and has a more bulbous body than the taper style. These decanters are usually engraved with floral motifs or fruiting vines: this one (*c.*1770) has a facet-cut neck and base with an engraved monogram.
£400–500/$650–800

STYLES OF STOPPER & DECANTER

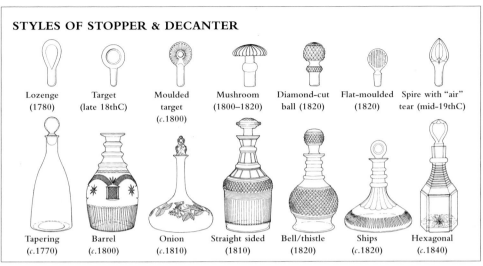

Lozenge (1780)

Target (late 18thC)

Moulded target (c.1800)

Mushroom (1800–1820)

Diamond-cut ball (1820)

Flat-moulded (1820)

Spire with "air" tear (mid-19thC)

Tapering (c.1770)

Barrel (c.1800)

Onion (c.1810)

Straight sided (1810)

Bell/thistle (1820)

Ships (c.1820)

Hexagonal (c.1840)

▶ **ENGRAVED LABEL**
Decanters with engraved labels, such as this piece (c.1790), reveal the popularity of certain wines at this time. The unusual horizontal ribbing around the body – a style known as Lynn glass – is very rare.
£1,500–2,500/
$2,400–4,000

◀ **BRISTOL BLUE**
In the 18th and early 19thC "Bristol" coloured-glass decanters were used for serving spirits, as their gilded labels – usually "rum", "brandy' and "hollands" (gin) – suggest. Blue is the colour most commonly found.
£1,500–2,000/
$2,400–3,200

◀ **SAILING SHIPS**
This decanter is engraved with a picture of sailing ships, suggesting that it might have been made for presentation to a ship's captain or owner. The ovoid shape and target stopper are characteristic of 1780s designs. £700–900/$1,125–1,440

▶ **SHIP'S DECANTER**
Amethyst decanters are generally much rarer than the blue or green ones. The form of this plain piece (c.1800), with its wide, flat base, is a variant on the "Rodney" or ship's decanter. The applied neck rings make it easier to handle.
£650–750/$1,050–1,200

EARLY ENGLISH II

In contrast to the relatively restrained styles of English decanters dating from the first half of the 18thC, later Georgian and Victorian decanters feature greater use of cut, engraved and mould-blown decoration, dictated by the fashion for richer ornament with the emergence of the Regency style *c.*1805. In this period deep-cutting on both English and Irish glass was particularly fashionable, and the finest decanters were embellished all over with panels of relief or strawberry diamond-cut patterns, horizontal-cut bands and vertical-fluting. Pillar-cutting, featuring broad flutes cut in relief with rounded edges, was popular from 1820–40. Pillar-cutting on a curve is especially prized. Decanter shapes became heavier, with wide and stout bodies and shorter necks, in contrast to earlier styles. Coloured decanters also became more popular from the 1830s with the fashion for hock and other German white wines.

▼ ANGLO-IRISH CUT GLASS
This ornate cut-glass "Anglo-Irish" decanter features strawberry diamond-cut panels on the body and a hollow-blown mushroom stopper. The decoration on the body and stopper should always match, showing that the two pieces were made at the same time and that the stopper is not a replacement.
£200–300/$325–475

▼ SPIRE-SHAPED STOPPER
The tall slender shape of this pale olive-green decanter (*c.*1835), made by the well-known firm of W.H., B. & J. Richardson, follows the shape of a hock bottle. The architectural form and spire shape of the stopper reflect the influence of the Gothic Revival style. £350–500/$560–800

▲ BRILLIANT CLARITY
The elegant tapering form of this decanter (*c.*1770), with a vertical disc stopper cut with simple facets round its edge, is characteristic of the plain styles of late 18thC decanters, left undecorated to show the colour of the wine and the brilliant clarity of the glass. Most decanters of this time have a capacity of a quart, but unusually this example holds a magnum.
£1,000–1,200/$1,600–1,920

◀ RARE INDIAN-CLUB DECANTER

Cutting is rarely found on decanters made before the 1760s, but it became increasingly popular through the late 18thC, culminating in the heavily cut styles of the Regency period. This rare Indian-club decanter has a facet-cut stopper and neck, with fluting around the base. The lozenge shape of the stopper is typical of the period, and the ground texture of the stopper peg should be matched by that inside the neck of the decanter. Signs of wear on the base of the decanter are also a good indication that the piece is a genuine one. £400–500/$650–800

◀ MANUFACTURER'S MARK

To create a decanter of standard capacity and shape involved blowing the gather of molten glass into a coaster-like mould. In the late 18thC and early 19thC some moulds, particularly Irish ones, featured the name of the manufacturer, which was incorporated into the base. Such pieces are very rare today: this one (c. 1800) is marked "Armstrong, Ormond Quay". £5,000–6,000/$8,000–9,600

▶ REGENCY STYLE

Ovoid shapes are characteristic of Regency decanters, made from the 1780s to the first decade of the 19thC. This example of c.1810 is of average quality, with restrained cutting: there are narrow-cut flutes around the base, broad fluting on the shoulders, and the stopper – an early 19thC mushroom shape – is star cut. The neck rings, made separately and applied to the body, make the decanter easier to handle. £200–300/$325–475

▶ REGENCY COPIES

Revivals of the Regency style in the 1880s and the 1930s led to the manufacture of many copies of late 18th and early 19thC decanters. The slightly clumsy form and bright, rather than grey, tone of the glass mark this one (c.1880) as a copy. Originals have more concave lines to the shoulders, are not rounded around the bases, and never feature "hat"-shaped stoppers. Copies from the 1930s can also be identified by neck rings that are moulded out of the body rather than made separately. £150–200/$240–325

LATER ENGLISH I

Mid-19thC decanters were produced in a very broad range of styles, to cater to all tastes and pockets – and are also still widely available today. The lingering influence of heavy Regency styles can be seen in the continued use of neck rings and cutting – much less fashionable after the Great Exhibition – but the Victorian fascination with the past is evident in such features as spire-shaped stoppers inspired by the contemporary interest in medieval Gothic art. Decoration varied from engraved and acid-etched patterns to more complex coloured overlay, especially on the tall narrow decanters in the style of hock bottles. However, in the second half of the 19thC there was a reaction against ornate decoration led by the critic John Ruskin (1819–1900) – who maintained that "all cut glass is barbarous" – leading to the development of simpler, much plainer forms.

◀ **"NELSON" STYLE**
Often described as
a "Nelson" decanter,
this piece (*c.*1830)
has a much more
elaborate shape than
earlier ones. The body
is also much heavier
than on 18thC examples,
but the hollow-blown
mushroom stopper and
three neck rings are the
last remaining vestiges
of Georgian style.
£100–200/$160–325

▶ **MID-CENTURY STYLE**
The rounded form
and neck rings of this
*c.*1840s decanter show
the influence of earlier
designs, but the vertical
emphasis and spire-
shaped stopper are
typical of those made
in the 1840s and 1850s.
The body is cut with
large printies or facets –
some more ornate
examples feature a
combination of cutting
and engraving, very
rarely found on 18thC
work. Decanters like
this are quite common.
£100–200/$160–325

▶ **WATERLILIES**
From 1850–1900 the
shaft-and-globe shape
of decanter, with a long
neck and rounded body,
was popular. Engraving
was the preferred form
of decoration – this 1860
example has a waterlily
design, then a favourite
motif. The overall effect
is much lighter than
earlier styles.
£350–500/$560–800

COLLECTING POINTS
• Pairs of decanters are particularly rare and can fetch up to three times as much as a single decanter.
• Genuine antique decanters should show signs of wear on the base through use.
• Decoration on the stopper should match that on the body on cut or engraved decanters.

◄ PALL MALL PATTERN
This decanter (*c.*1880) is acid-etched with a design of circles known as the "Pall Mall" pattern. Although a good piece, the pattern is associated with later, poorly made glass, making a plain decanter worth more. £100–200/$160–325

► WHITE WINE DECANTER
This 1870 example is made of cased glass, revealing clear glass underneath – cheaper versions, with much thinner outer layers, were flashed. Coloured shaft-and-globe decanters, especially green ones, are rare. £350–500/$560–800

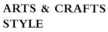

ARTS & CRAFTS STYLE

Late 19thC design reformers, especially members of the Arts and Crafts Movement, believed that glassware should reflect the intrinsic beauty of the material and advocated much simpler, almost minimalist, forms for decanters and other tableware. The firm of James Powell and Sons of London is associated with this style of "pumpkin seed" decanter. £200–300/$325–475

The stopper was probably blown into the same mould as the body of the decanter.

Decoration is either extremely restrained or absent, so that the transparency of the material was emphasized.

The austere, almost geometric form is characteristic of Arts and Crafts decanters.

Simple moulded feet are common, to add visual balance and increase the amount of light reflected through the glass.

The body is generally very light in weight and thinly blown – later copies are much heavier in feel.

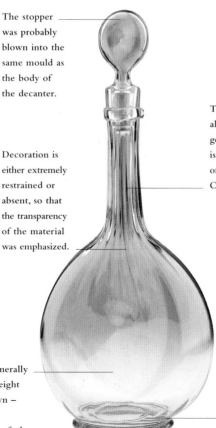

LATER ENGLISH II

By the late 19thC decanters in a enormous range of styles and forms were being produced in England, usually as part of large matching table services. Decorated decanters were available at modest prices, mainly as a result of considerable technical innovations: steam-powered cutting wheels enabled the manufacture of all-over deeply-cut ornament, while in the 1860s a machine for mechanically reproducing patterns on glass for acid-etching was invented, further reducing production costs. However, manufacturers in Stourbridge maintained their reputation as the leaders in the production of luxury glass decanters and other tableware, and were particularly renowned for their use of rock crystal and intaglio engraving on their best, top-of-the-range, pieces. Silver mounts, which were first used on claret jugs in the 1860s, are also a distinctive feature of decanters made from the 1880s up until the beginning of World War I in 1914.

▶ **INTAGLIO ENGRAVING**
The flattened form of this amethyst cased-glass decanter with silver mounts (1896) is generally described as "mandolin" shape. A Stevens & Williams piece, it is intaglio-engraved with a pattern of flowers and scrolls within woven basketwork – the three-dimensional effect is a sign of very fine craftsmanship.
£4,000–6,000/$6,400–9,600

▼ **SILVER MOUNTS**
This cut-glass decanter with silver mounts (1908) is typical of pieces of average quality made from c.1880–c.1914: the style of cutting is rather old-fashioned and unimaginative, while the mounts are plain – more expensive items have engraved or embossed mounts. The small size indicates that the decanter was made for spirits, such as whisky. £250–350/$400–560

◀ **MADE FOR EXPORT**
Many elaborate services were made in England in the late 19thC for wealthy Americans: this decanter, which features a combination of cutting and rock-crystal engraved panels, was part of a suite of over 300 pieces made for the tycoon J. J. Gould.
£1,200–1,800/$1,920–2,880

▶ **SHAFT AND GLOBE**
This amethyst cased-glass
decanter is a fairly late example
of a coloured shaft-and-globe
decanter. The flattened shape
dates it to *c.*1900. Decanters in
this style, with simple engraved
patterns, are still made today.
Modern pieces have a bright,
"chemical" look, as opposed
to the jewel-like colours of the
19thC. £150–250/$240–400

▲ **SIGNED PIECE**
Most late 19thC suites of glass
were made with optional claret
jugs. Today these are less
common in pristine condition
than are decanters as the handles
are vulnerable. This engraved
piece (1870) has a signature, but

nothing is known of the engraver
other than his name – Wilson.
Signatures on engraving add to
the value but should always be
treated with caution – check
that the wording is engraved
into the glass and not acid-
etched. £350–500/$560–800

SILVER MOUNTS
Silver mounts on decanters
and claret jugs were
popular at the end of the
19thC. They are secured
with plaster and can be
useful in dating pieces, as
they should be hallmarked.
Always check the date, as
many jugs and decanters
in this style are still being
produced, and that the
mount fits tightly around
the neck – a good sign
that it is an original piece.

▶ **HOCK-BOTTLE SHAPE**
Intaglio-engraved with a pattern
of fruiting vines (possibly by
Joshua Hodgetts), this hock-
bottle-shaped decanter, made
by Stevens & Williams *c.*1900,
has three coloured layers –
clear, red and yellow –
technically much harder to
achieve than the usual two
coloured layers because
each layer cools at a different
rate during manufacture.
£2,000–3,000/$3,200–4,800

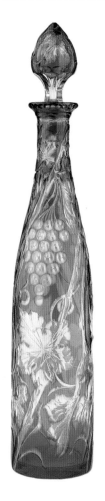

BOHEMIAN

In central Europe early decanters were frequently made as part of travelling sets. The bottles usually had screw tops, and were designed to fit snugly into a travelling box. These boxes were meant to hold several decanters – sometimes as many as eight – but normally only two glasses. The wealthy traveller and his companion were thus assured of a selection of warming drinks throughout the journey and when they stopped to rest for the night. During the early 19thC a fashion for English crystal swept across Europe, and Bohemian glass factories lost no time in producing copies of the more popular styles. These imitations were made in soda glass and thus were often lighter than the originals, but the cutting is usually more ornate, in accordance with Bohemian taste.

◀ RED FLASHED DECANTER
Although the reputation of Bohemian glass was enhanced by the superb quality of the metal, highly skilled decorative techniques and superior craftsmanship, not all products produced at the glassworks of Bohemia could claim to be worthy of such high distinction. This decanter (c.1830) has been flashed in red and then rather crudely decorated with shallow engraving through the colour in an effort to give the illusion of an expensive overlay.
£400–450/$650–725

▶ RARE SCREW TOP
This screw-top travelling decanter (c.1760) is a highly unusual piece, as it is generally believed that the mechanism of internal screw threads on glass was not invented until the late 19thC. This early and very rare screw-top decanter has been engraved with foliage, a design found on other large Bohemian glasses and tumblers. The screw top has been cut in the shape of a bull's eye, a style also frequently used for stoppers on British decanters produced in the Georgian period.
£450–500/ $725–800

▲ BOHEMIAN COPY OF ENGLISH STYLE
This Bohemian copy of an English decanter was made in the early 19thC. Like those of many Bohemian copies, the shape of the decanter mirrors the English styles, but the cutting is more ornate to accommodate Bohemian taste.
£150–200/$240–325

◀ TRAVELLER'S JOY
The expensive gilded decoration on this travelling bottle has been confined to the shoulders and neck, the only parts visible when the decanter was tucked into its travelling box. Decanters like this one usually had ball or peg-shaped stoppers, which were small enough to allow for a snug-fitting lid. £750–800/$1,200–1,275

HARRACHOV GLASSWORKS

Founded in 1712 at Novy Svet in northern Bohemia, this company was known for its high quality glassware. In 1887 it was acquired by Josef Riedel, whose family had developed *Annagrün* and *Annagelb* glass in the 1840s. Riedel produced luxury decorated pieces that were widely exported.

AUGUST BOHM

This engraved blue-stained decanter (*c.*1845–50) has been signed by August Bohm, one of the most accomplished Bohemian glass engravers from the Biedermeier period. The engraving features the Madonna and Child seated in a landscape. The bottle is a type of decanter that was produced at the Stourbridge glass factories in England, where Bohm is known to have worked at this time. £4,000–4,500/ $6,400–7,200

▲ REGENCY INFLUENCE
This Bohemian decanter (*c.*1820), made of soda glass, reflects the contemporary style of the Regency period in England. The gilding and engraved decoration which were typical of 18thC decanters have been replaced by heavy cutting. The decanter's large bulbous body, neck rings, short neck for easy handling, and mushroom-shaped stopper are all decorative features typical of Regency design. £300–350/ $475–560

FRENCH

The fashion for using decanters to serve wine at the dining table was adopted in France at the beginning of the 19thC. This trend coincided with the new enthusiasm in France for English crystal glass. Many French and Belgian glass factories employed itinerant English and Irish workers, and the decanters produced there were inevitably strongly influenced by the Anglo-Irish styles, with their elegant forms and high-quality craftsmanship. Later in the century, the passion for all things English was followed by an essentially "French" style, with the emphasis on colour, gilding and, occasionally, enamelled decoration (unlike early Anglo-Irish cut glass examples, which are never gilded or enamelled). French decanters tend to be considerably larger or smaller than their English counterparts; the latter commonly hold a standard measure of two imperial pints (just over one litre), while some French decanters can hold a magnum.

▶ MAGNUM DECANTER

This magnum crystal decanter, made at the Vonêche Glassworks (c.1810–20), was produced by itinerant Irish glassworkers. The style of cutting strongly resembles typical Irish technique, but the shape of the decanter is not British. This example holds 1.5 litres (a magnum). £850–900/ $1,360–1,450

▼ ST LOUIS CLARET JUG

This late 19thC claret jug by the St Louis factory exhibits the "French" style in glassware that had developed by the second half of the 19thC. The fashion for British designs was superseded by an imaginative use of colours and fine gilding that particularly appealed to French taste. £475–525/$750–850

◀ FRENCH DECANTER IN THE ENGLISH STYLE

Decanters like this rather poor copy of an English style (c.1820) were produced at glassworks throughout Europe. The inferior colour of the metal indicates that this barrel-shaped example is most likely to be French. £400–450/$650–725

◀ BLUE-AND-WHITE SWIRL
The shape of this blue-and-white swirl carafe (*c*.1850) mirrors exactly the style of English decanters from the late 18thC. Made of high-quality crystal by the celebrated St Louis Glassworks in Alsace, it has been decorated with a fanciful pattern influenced by Venetian designs. It is extremely rare to find large pieces such as this one, which have been decorated with a technique more commonly used for paperweights.
£600–650/$950–1,050

▶ FLAMBOYANT CUTTING
The design of this crystal decanter (*c*.1835) exhibits strong Anglo-Irish influence, but the heavy, flamboyant cutting style identifies it as an early product of the renowned Baccarat factory. This fine example reflects the superb quality of glassware produced by Baccarat since the mid-18thC.
£300–375/$475–600

▶ LATE 19THC GILDED DECANTER
Although this pretty glass decanter made at the end of the 19thC resembles the popular styles produced at the Baccarat and St Louis factories, the poor quality of the metal and the inferior workmanship betray it as a lacklustre imitation. French decanters were often made of coloured glass – usually blue – and were frequently decorated with gilding, as on this example. Enamelling was another popular form of decoration for decanters, but such examples are quite rare.
£180–200/$290–325

VONÊCHE GLASSWORKS
The innovative Vonêche Glassworks in Belgium, established in 1778 near Namur by a Frenchman, employed many Irish glassworkers. The factory produced elaborate lead-crystal wares in the English style from 1802 to 1830, including vases, goblets, dishes and clockcases. Many of the most ornate designs were created by the talented glassworker, Charpentier, who worked at Vonêche before going on to establish the firm of Escalier de Cristal, based in Paris.

AMERICAN

American-made decanters found today date mainly from the 19thC and early 20thC and were produced in a wide variety of colours and styles. While some early American glass decanters copy English cut-glass styles, many pieces are narrower and more bottle-like in shape, perhaps inspired by the vast quantities of plain and practical glass bottles used for storing wine and spirits in the newly established communities of the Midwest. Mould-blowing and, especially, press-moulding were the most popular methods for making inexpensive yet decorative decanters, with often elaborate patterns created as an integral part of the body. More luxurious decanters were made at the end of the 19thC and include coloured items with naturalistic decoration in silver overlay. Decanters and jugs in an Art Deco geometric style, many with matching glasses, were produced during the 1930s, in line with the current fashion for bolder, abstract forms.

◀ "DIAMOND THUMBPRINT"
This Boston & Sandwich 1850s decanter in the "diamond thumbprint" pattern is made in pressed lead glass. The Boston & Sandwich Glass Co. was so closely associated with pressed-glass manufacture that much American pressed glass is now often called "Sandwich glass".
£125–250/$200–400

CARNIVAL GLASS
This is inexpensive press-moulded glassware with an iridescent finish made by spraying the hot glass with metallic salts, in the style of luxury art glass by Tiffany. It was made from the 1890s to the 1920s by firms such as the Imperial Glass Co. at Bellaire, Ohio, and Harry Northwood at Indiana, Pennsylvania.

◀ "WASHINGTON" PATTERN
This "Washington" pattern decanter in lead glass was produced by the New England Glass Co. of East Cambridge, Massachusetts c.1869. Like all lead-glass decanters, it should show signs of wear on the base and have a clear ring when tapped. The decoration on the stopper should always match that on the main body of the decanter.
£125–250/$200–400

▼ "OCTAGON" PATTERN

This marigold "Octagon" Carnival Glass decanter (*c.* 1920) by the Imperial Glass Co. at Bellaire, Ohio, was produced with matching glasses for serving sherry and other sweet wines. Sets in amethyst-coloured glass are also known but are much rarer. Brightly coloured American-made Carnival Glass was exported to Britain in large quantities between the wars. £175–250/$280–400

▶ INNOVATIVE SHAPE

This etched glass decanter with an inventive circular shape was made by the Pairpoint Manufacturing Company, one of the leading American glass manufacturers at the turn of the 19thC. Pairpoint was better known for its "Puffy" lamps with mould-blown glass shades in high relief, hand-painted on the inside with flowers such as roses and pansies. £425–550/$700–900

▼ COCKTAIL SET

The plain tapering cylindrical form of the glasses and the angular handle on the stoppered decanter of this cocktail set made by the Steuben Glass Works are characteristic of the Art Deco era. Decoration of simple black threading, inspired by Venetian glass, was also common. £250–375/$400–600

STEUBEN GLASS

The Steuben Glass Works, established in 1903, became famed for its high-quality iridescent gold and blue "Aurene" art-glass vases. After 1934 the firm specialized in elegant tableware and ornamental wares. Most pieces are signed "Steuben" – either acid-etched, engraved, in script or on a paper label.

Jugs

Glass jugs, largely intended for religious rituals, are known from ancient Rome, although complete examples from this period are rare. In the 15thC and 16thC some elaborate jugs and ewers with globular bodies, often embellished with hinged lids and thumbpieces in precious metals, were created as luxury items for display or exchanged as diplomatic gifts. It was not until the early 19thC, when technical advances permitted the production of reasonably priced glass tableware, that practical, utilitarian glass jugs were introduced. A variety of shapes can be found, including globular, conical, ovoid and cylindrical, all with a pouring lip or spout and a loop handle on the opposite side, and sometimes a stopper in the style of contemporary decanters. Jugs were made for serving both wine and water – the latter usually have a much wider neck suitable for frequent refilling – and for display; some fine European pieces feature elaborate enamelling, cutting and engraving. Jugs with matching pairs of goblets were popular in the Victorian era as wedding gifts, and as part of larger table services. Jugs in pristine condition are rarer today than decanters, mainly because the addition of a handle to the cooling glass body during manufacture created weakness in the piece, leading to cracks. The pouring lip was also vulnerable, and the inside of the vessel, if heavily used, may be cloudy from water damage. When buying glass jugs always check for damage around the lip and where the handle joins the body.

WATER JUGS 18th–19thC

Glass water jugs first appeared around 1800, when there was increasing demand for matching sets of glass tableware. Before this water and beer – consumed by the majority but disregarded by the wealthy – were usually served in pottery jugs. In the early 19thC changes in dining etiquette, as well as improvements in water quality and the introduction of mass-produced glassware, meant that water jugs were now seen in middle-class homes. In the Victorian era there were many styles, from relatively expensive, engraved pieces to sturdier, plain or simply etched jugs for use in bars and taverns.

◀ 1850s STYLE

While the heavy cutting on this jug of c.1850 is characteristic of Georgian jugs, the curvaceous shape of the body, handle and pouring rim, and the scrolling form of the rim, date it to the mid-19thC – after the 1850s there was a change in taste, with lighter engraving instead of cutting.
£100–200/$160–325

▶ IRISH DESIGN

This jug (c.1820), with a curving neck and more cylindrical body, is more formal in style than the jug of c.1790–1800 – and probably formed part of a service. Jugs of the time nearly always hold 2 or 3 pints. The pillar-cutting around the body was popular in the 1820s.
£300–400/$475–650

IRISH JUG

In the late 18thC and early 19thC glass manufacture expanded rapidly in Ireland – as a result of the emigration of many leading English glassmakers due to the heavy taxes on glass in England. Irish glasshouses are associated with cut glass, particularly pieces combining different patterns of cutting. This Irish jug (c.1790–1800) is quite restrained, with shallow cutting around the body. £350–500/$560–800

Good-quality cutting adds to the value.

The very wide neck indicates that the jug was made for water or beer.

Jugs are rarer today than decanters because the handles are vulnerable.

The squat, rounded shape is characteristic of Irish designs.

On jugs made before c.1870 the handle was attached just under the rim and drawn down.

▲ MASS PRODUCTION
Coloured glass jugs were mass-produced in the 19thC. Like contemporary drinking glasses, which combined coloured bowls with clear stems, this jug of c.1870 has a cranberry body, engraved with ferns, and a clear handle. £150–250/$240–400

▼ UTILITARIAN MODEL
Simply decorated straight-sided jugs were made by the thousand from the 1870s until 1914, and are still fairly easy to find. Some were engraved, like this jug (c.1880), but the engraving lacks the depth of cutting and detail found on more expensive pieces. £100–150/$160–240

▲ ACID-ETCHED PIECE
This jug (c.1880) is similar in style to the engraved piece but has acid-etched decoration. Such jugs were made in 1, 2, or 3-pint sizes, but the single-pint version is rarer than the larger ones. They were made mainly for use in bars and hotels. £100–150/$160–240

ENGLISH & IRISH WINE JUGS

There is a longer tradition of glass jugs specifically made for serving wine than for water jugs: before the early 19thC both glass and wine were expensive commodities that only the wealthy could afford. Like water and beer jugs, wine jugs were, however, increasingly made as part of larger table services, or with goblets as presentation sets, from the beginning of the Victorian era; clear glass jugs were intended for claret and red wines, in order to show off the colour of the wine, while coloured-glass pieces were used for serving white wines and champagne. Most 19thC jugs follow the style of contemporary decanters, but have added handles, pouring lips and sometimes larger stoppers. Wine jugs are rarer than decanters, mainly as the addition of a handle created stresses in the glass body during manufacture, often resulting in breakage. Shapes developed from simple lines to more ornate and heavy forms later in the century.

▶ **THREE CUTTING STYLES**
This jug (c.1810) combines styles of cutting – a star-cut base, step-cutting on the neck and diamond-cutting on the body – characteristic of good Irish Regency glass. Unlike later pieces, early jugs usually came without stoppers. If there is a slight ridge inside the neck, and if the neck is narrower than a thumb's width, there should be one. £600–800/ $950–1,275

▲ **IRISH JUG**
The wide body and gently curving shoulders of this Irish wine jug (c.1810) is similar to decanters of the period, as is the use of pillar cutting on the body. Good-quality Regency jugs are particularly valuable today as many have been damaged through handling, with chips or cracks in the rims and broken handles. Tapping the handle lightly may indicate whether it has been damaged – it should ring if in perfect condition. £800–1,200/$1,275–1,925

◀ **MID-VICTORIAN PIECE**
The taller, elongated body and high-looped handle of this jug date it to c.1850. The cutting and engraving are lighter in style than on Regency pieces, and are characteristic of jugs made from the mid-19thC. As on water jugs, the handle was first applied at the top of the body and then drawn down, as shown by the thickness of the handle just below the rim. £700–1,000/$1,125–1,600

LOOKING AFTER A WINE JUG

While jugs that are cloudy inside should be avoided, as this indicates water damage, dirt can simply be removed by gently brushing with a bottle brush and warm soapy water. The jug should then be dried thoroughly with a soft cloth to prevent staining. Wine or spirit stains can be dissolved by using a bleach solution. Glass with more serious stains should be taken to an expert. Always support the body of a jug when cleaning or handling – do not hold it by the handle.

▶ CLASSICAL INSPIRATION

With the popularity of the Grecian style in the 1870s, jugs were often produced in shapes derived from ancient vases, like this piece of c.1870. Most were engraved with simple Greek-key patterns, but the best examples – largely produced for the many international exhibitions of the time – feature linear engraved or etched designs adapted from Greek sculpture or pottery. £1,000–1,200/ $1,600–1,925

◀ GIFT SET

This jug (c.1860) was made as part of a service with two large matching goblets. Such sets were often given as presentation pieces and are described on manufacturers' lists as sets for serving lemonade or champagne – during the 19thC champagne was decanted and so was rather flatter in taste than it is today.

◀ BULBOUS SHAPE

This jug of c.1880 is representative of the move away from relatively simple classically-inspired forms to the more bulbous and ornate shapes of the later 19thC – the curved rim, for example, is more pronounced than on earlier jugs.

Modestly priced, acid-etched jugs, often with matching goblets, were produced from the 1870s and 1880s to meet the ever-increasing demand for inexpensive, practical yet attractive glassware, and can still be reasonably priced today. £250–350/$400–560

CENTRAL EUROPEAN

The earliest glass jugs made in central Europe during the 16thC and 17thC, often with silver, silver-gilt or even gold mounts and hinged lids, were intended as luxury items for display or to be exchanged as important diplomatic or court gifts. During the 18thC and 19thC, however, a number of fine-quality clear-glass jugs embellished with sophisticated engraving – a speciality of central European and especially Bohemian glassmaking – appeared, in response to the growing demand of the middle classes for elegant tableware. Jugs were also produced in the novel coloured, marbled "Lithyalin" glass developed by the Bohemian Friedrich Egermann (1777–1864), while the *Historismus* movement in 19thC Germany harked back to the 16thC and 17thC. Although 19thC forms of jug are similar to those made elsewhere in Europe, Bohemian pieces can be identified by the exceptionally high standard of their decorative engraving and enamelling.

BOHEMIAN GLASS ENGRAVERS

Some of the most prominent 19thC glass engravers were Bohemian. They include Dominik Biemann (1800–57), August Bohm (1812–90), and the Sachr and Pohl families. Many engravers worked all over Europe and even in the USA.

▶ FORMALIZED ENGRAVING

Like that of many forms of glassware, the style of this German jug (*c*.1750), with its large bulbous body, elegantly curving handle and rudimentary foot, was derived from examples in silver and not pottery, as during this period glass was still considered a luxury commodity as expensive as precious metal. The formalized pattern of scrolls and flowers is characteristic of central European glass engraving from 1750 to 1800. £700–900/$1,125–1,440

◀ GERMAN WATER JUG

This German jug of *c*.1780 shows the influence of English and Irish glass in the simple cutting around the base, but the formal all-over engraving is distinctively Continental. The wide neck suggests that it may have been used for serving water or ale rather than wine. As with English jugs, the manufacture of the handle is a good indication of date – before the late 19thC the handle was applied at the neck and drawn down onto the body. Like the other 18thC jug shown here, this jug is made of potash-lime glass – a type of potash glass with chalk added in the batch to improve its refractive qualities. £700–900/$1,125–1,440

◀ LOBMEYR JUG
The Lobmeyr factory in Austria, founded by Josef Lobmeyr in 1822, was the leading maker of fine-quality glass in a variety of exotic and historical styles in 19thC central Europe: the engraving on the body of this magnum wine jug *c.*1870 is inspired by 17thC Baroque patterns. Other wares produced by the firm at this time include goblets with enamelled decoration combining Islamic script and Renaissance motifs. £800–1,000/$1,275–1,600

▶ FLUID STYLE
During the early 19thC glass-enamelling workshops were established by Samuel Mohn (1762–1815) in Leipzig and Dresden, and by Anton Kothgasser (1769–1851) in Vienna. Here, the soft fluid style of the enamelled flowers and birds on a white background is inspired by the work of these men. £1,200–1,500/$1,925–2,400

▶ *HISTORISMUS*
The copying of antique German glassware – a movement known as *Historismus* – was popular in central Europe following the unification of Germany in 1871. Like this 19thC jug, these wares are generally pale yellowish-green or amber, and are decorated with bright enamels, sometimes of fictitious coats of arms. £300–500/$475–800

OTHER

While clear-glass jugs are generally practical serving vessels, many larger jugs, bottles and flasks were, like vases, used as vehicles for the display of virtuoso glass craftsmanship. Among the earliest examples are the diamond-point engraved pieces decorated in The Netherlands and Belgium in the 17thC by craftsmen such as Willem Mooleyser (c.1640–1700); in the 19thC fine-quality jugs made throughout Europe and the USA feature cutting,

engraving and coloured-glass decoration – glass claret jugs were also made with fine silver or plated mounts and handles. In contrast to these luxury pieces – and more affordable today – are the more practical, sturdy jugs made of bottle glass at provincial English factories, and the colourful pressed-glass pitchers produced in the early 20thC by both English and American manufacturers, often with matching sets of drinking glasses.

◀ RARE
DUTCH FLASK
Some of the finest diamond-point engraved glassware was executed by Dutch craftsmen in the 17thC and 18thC. This rare flask with a silver-mounted cork stopper features detailed diamond-point engraving of hawks, flowers and flying insects, among foliage. £8,000–12,000/ $12,800–19,200

◀ LARGE JUG
This large, two-gallon jug, made by the Wrockwardine Wood glasshouse in Shropshire, was most likely used at public gatherings. In the early 19thC this company specialized in bottle glass embellished with splashes of white or coloured glass, making wares similar in style to Nailsea bells, flasks, and other small items. £800–1,200/ $1,280–2,000

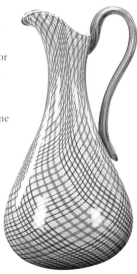

▶ ST LOUIS EWER
In the mid-19thC the French glassworks of St Louis was known for its fine *latticinio* wares. Many of these consist of a clear glass body worked with a very fine lattice of fine pink or blue and white canes, but this ewer (c.1860) has a body of opaque white glass overlaid in blue and pink in a chequered spiralling thread pattern. £1,500– 2,500/$2,400–4,000

▶ "SLUG" JUG
The angular shape of this American jug (c.1880) derives from Russian silverware and is called a "slug" jug. It is made of "amberina", a type of heat-sensitive coloured glass developed by Joseph Locke at the New England Glass Co. and patented in 1883, though later made by other factories. £400–600/$640–960

◀ BACCARAT DOLPHIN WINE JUG

This valuable, richly carved wine jug (c.1860) in the shape of a dolphin is typical of the extravagant style of cut and engraved luxury glassware made at the Baccarat factory in France during the Victorian era. Such items are almost too heavy for practical use, even when empty, and so were probably intended as decorative items in wealthy households, or for display at the many international exhibitions of the time. £2,000–3,000/ $3,200–4,800

▶ IRISH JUG

This magnificent crystal jug (c.1805– 10) is a fine example of Irish cut glass, and would probably have been made as an expensive gift or a presentation piece. Unusually, it has ormolu or gilt-bronze mounts, based on a pattern by the well- known Birmingham silversmith and ormolu-maker Matthew Boulton. Most items with ormolu mounts were made in France. £4,000–6,000/ $6,400–9,600

Check that the plaster securing the mount to the glass body is secure.

The combination of step-cutting around the neck and diamond- cutting on the body is typically Irish.

The finely detailed scrolling style of the handle will add to the value of the piece.

The elegant ovoid form is inspired by ancient Greek and Roman pottery vases and is typical of the late 18thC and early 19thC Neo-classical style.

◀ DEPRESSION JUG

This press-moulded green-glass pitcher, with a curved-in lip to trap ice cubes, is typical of the inexpensive mechanically-produced tableware, known as "Depression" glass, made in the USA during the 1930s. Most of these pieces were made of coloured or translucent glass, but some clear and opaque examples may be found. Much of this glass is angular in style. £40–55/$65–90

Vases

Made in every variety of style, shape and ornament, vases are among the most popular items of glassware with collectors today. Most available pieces date from the 19thC and early 20thC – the most productive period of technical and artistic innovation in glassmaking. Vases specifically for holding flowers were only really introduced at the end of the 19thC, with the vogue for exotic flowers that arrived with the interest in Japanese art. Many earlier vases were made in pairs, to sit on either side of a mantelpiece, and often had covers – typical of these ornate pieces are those made in France, in coloured or opaline glass with ormolu mounts, often of classical motifs. Elaborate centrepieces known as épergnes – consisting of several decorative glass sections attached to or slotted into metal frames – also appeared in the late 19thC and were intended to hold impressive floral displays. Being decorative rather than functional, vases and épergnes were the perfect vehicle for manufacturers to show off their skills in producing the unusual surface treatments and colours, elaborate shapes and ornate applied decoration, typical of the so-called "art" and "fancy" glass – ornamental blown and pressed wares – made from the 1870s in Europe and the USA. US firms are especially associated with experiments in iridescence, and some of the Favrile vases created by the Tiffany Glass & Decorating Co. are among the most highly priced on the market today. At the same time, simpler practical pieces such as celery vases, a part of matching sets of tableware, were made.

ENGLISH

The heyday of the English vase was from c.1850 to c.1900, a period in which many firms experimented with coloured, enamelled and silvered glass, producing virtuoso pieces especially for the Great Exhibition of 1851 at the Crystal Palace. The highest quality and most sophisticated pieces were made by the leading Midlands manufacturers of luxury tableware, including W. H., B. and J. Richardson, George Bacchus & Sons, Stevens & Williams and Thomas Webb & Sons. Initially designs were somewhat restrained – often taking inspiration from ancient Greek and Roman Classical style – but from the 1870s ornate trailed and pincered forms and often vibrant colours were fashionable.

◄ ORNATE EPERGNE
This ivory opal-glass épergne was made c.1875 by Stevens & Williams. The crimped edges and ruby-glass trailing on the rims of each section are typical of art and fancy glass made from the 1870s until 1914. Always check that an épergne is complete – holes in the base or holder indicate missing parts. £1,750–2,250/$2,800–3,600

EPERGNES
In the 18thC épergnes comprised metal frames with glass or silver dishes intended to hold sweetmeats and fruit, but in the following century they were popular as flower holders.

SILVERED GLASS

In 1849 Edward Varnish and Frederick Hale Thomson patented a way of lining a double-walled glass vessel with silver to produce mirror-like glass. Much silvered glass is plain, but some pieces used coloured glass and were embellished with cutting or engraving, like these blue-cased cylindrical vases (*c.*1850), intaglio-cut with a band of diamond trellis. Silvered glass was popular in England for a short time around 1850, but poor-quality copies were made later. £400–500/$650–950 (each)

◀ **CELERY VASE**

This pillar-moulded vase of *c.*1840 was made to hold celery to be eaten with cheese. Celery vases were generally only made in England, from about 1800 until the 20thC. They are a characteristically wide, flared, stemmed form and were usually made in clear glass. £120–180/$190–290

◀ **ART NOUVEAU**

The late 19thC craze for Japanese art led to vast imports of exotic flowers. They were best displayed in tall narrow vases like this 1.35m (4ft) vaseline-glass vase (*c.*1900). The plant-like form and flower-shaped rim are typical of Art Nouveau work. £2,500–3,500/ $4,000–5,600

▶ **VASELINE GLASS**

Like the lily vase above right, this late 19thC vase was made of opalescent "Vaseline" glass, so-called because of the slightly greasy look of its surface. Characteristic shades include blue, yellow and green. The somewhat austere form of this vase illustrates the trend towards much simpler styles at the end of the 19thC. £300–500/ $475–800

▶ **CLASSICAL STYLE**

This white opaline-glass vase of *c.*1850, made by George Bacchus & Sons, illustrates the fashion for classical themes around the time of the Great Exhibition. Unusually for this date it is marked with the maker's name. £700–900/$1,125–1,440

CONTINENTAL

In continental Europe the most innovative glass vases were produced in France and Bohemia during the 19thC. Such vases are often in a style very different from that of contemporary English pieces – frequently inspired by ornamental wares in luxury materials such as porcelain and hardstones – but, as in England, proved to be the best medium for exploring new developments in glass technology, particularly colouring. Bohemian glassmakers were the leaders in the development of new colours: for example, in 1829 Friedrich Egermann patented his marbled "Lithyalin" glass imitating natural agate, and in the 1830s Josef Riedel developed yellow and green-toned glass by adding small amounts of uranium to the batch. In France many fine-quality vases were produced in opaline glass, a translucent white glass made with the addition of gold oxide, which has a fiery orange-red tint when it is held up to the light.

▼ NATURALISTIC BIRDS AND PLANTS This pair of richly painted French enamelled and gilded opaline vases of *c*.1850 are characteristic of the highest-quality opaline vases which were made in France during the mid-19thC. The decorative enamelling within an oval scrolled framework against a blue ground is inspired by contemporary French Sèvres porcelain. The finely detailed, naturalistically painted exotic birds and plants are among the most desirable subjects. £4,000–5,000/ $6,400–8,000

▲ FRENCH EMPIRE This amethyst-tinted vase (*c*.1840), cut with bands of diamonds and stylized leaves, would have been one of pair or part of a garniture – a set of three, five or seven pieces. The classically inspired design and the swan-shaped ormolu handles derive from the French Empire style of the Napoleonic period. £7,000–9,000/ $11,200–14,400

▶ **JAPANESE CHRYSANTHEMUMS**
As in England, more restrained forms began to appear in Continental glassware towards the end of the 19thC, through the influence of reforming designers. This vase, coloured blue around the rim, is enamelled with a pattern of chrysanthemums –

a popular motif with the interest in Japanese art which was so fashionable at the time. Other examples feature poppies, daisies and freesias. Such items are more accessible today to collectors than the earlier French opaline vases. £350–500/ $560–800

HYALITH GLASS
In the early 19thC the popularity of Wedgwood's red and black ceramic stoneware led the Count von Buquoy to develop this dense opaque black or red glass in 1819. It was used for vases and bowls and was usually gilded.

◀ **ELABORATE BOHEMIAN WORK**
Bohemian glassmakers were the pioneers in the development of casing, overlay, flashing and staining techniques for colouring glass in the 19thC. This overlay Bohemian vase is further embellished with gilding and enamelled flowers, and is typical of the very ornate styles, often combining several decorative techniques, made in Bohemia from 1840 to 1890. £300–400/$475–650

▶ **SIMULATED ONYX**
This French white-opaline vase, gilded and fitted with an ormolu-and-marble mount, was intended to simulate onyx. The mount is marked with the name and address of the Paris maker of the mount. As well as white, opaline glass was made in many colours, in particular a turquoise blue. Bohemian and English glassmakers also produced opaline glass from the mid-19thC, but their wares lack the rich opalescence of French pieces. £200–250/$325–400

AMERICAN

From the late 19thC many American glassmakers turned their attention from domestic tableware to the development of luxury art glass in a range of dazzling colours created by unusual techniques. Ornamental vases from this period are some of the best examples of American art glass. The leading exponent was Louis Comfort Tiffany (1848–1933), best known for his lamps with shades made of leaded panels of iridescent Favrile glass; he also produced a wide range of Art Nouveau vases of typically curving, sinuous shapes in iridescent and cameo glass, imitating the natural forms of plants and flowers. The popularity of Tiffany's wares meant that the manufacture of iridescent glass and other types of art glass was taken up by other firms, including the Quezal Art Glass & Decorating Company in Brooklyn, New York, and the Steuben Glass Works in Corning, New York.

▶ **CELERY VASE**
Tall vases for serving celery with cheese at the end of a meal were popular in the USA as well as Britain during the 19thC. This "Bellflower" pattern pressed-glass vase was produced by the Boston & Sandwich Glass Co. in the 1850s. Other US firms later produced the same pattern in non-lead glass. £125–185/$200–300

▼ **BRILLIANT CUTTING**
A style of rich, all-over complex cutting known as brilliant-cutting was first shown at the Philadelphia Centennial Exhibition in 1876. Most American brilliant-cut glass, such as this vase by T.G. Hawkes & Co. of Corning, New York, of c.1900, dates from c.1880 to 1915. Brilliant-cut glass should be heavy, with sharply defined cutting and signs of wear on the base; some pieces are signed with an acid-etched factory mark. £950–1,550/$1,500–2,500

◀ **"ROYAL FLEMISH" STYLE**
This unusual bottle-style vase (c.1890), based on Greco-Roman designs and enamelled to resemble stained glass, was made by the Mount Washington Glass Co. of Massachusetts. The pattern, made solely by Mount Washington from c.1890, is known as "Royal Flemish" (sometimes marked "RF") and features elaborate oriental, bird and flower motifs, as well as abstract designs. £5,000–7,500/$8,000–12,000

◀ TIFFANY FAVRILE GLASS

The Tiffany Glass and
Decorating Co. (as it was known
from 1892) is most closely
associated with iridescent Favrile
glass, which has a shimmering
surface reminiscent of that found
on long-buried ancient Roman
glass. This Favrile glass vase
(c.1913) has a typically elegant,
curving form with almost
abstract patterns reminiscent
of flowers. Similar vases with
a heavier textured surface were
made in "Cypriote" glass.
£3,750–6,250/$6,000–10,000

▶ VINELAND VASE

This elegant blue iridescent vase of the 1920s,
with a form somewhat similar to shaft-
and-globe decanters, was produced by the
Vineland Flint Glass Works at New Jersey,
owned by the French-born Victor Durand.
Vineland began to manufacture art glass in
1924 after the arrival of Martin Bach Jr.
(1865–1924), who first worked at Quezal.
Vineland wares are signed with the name
"Durand" in script or "Durand" superimposed
over a large "V", and are often known as
"Durand" vases. £1,250–1,875/$2,000–3,000

▶ STEUBEN "AURENE" VASE

At the Steuben Glass Works
in Corning, New York, the
English-born glassmaker
Frederick Carder developed
an innovative range of art
glass to compete with
Tiffany, including iridescent
"Aurene" glass as seen in this
1920s vase. Produced from
1904 to 1934, "Aurene" glass
is found in two main varieties –
gold and blue (the latter ranging
from pale and silvery to dark blue).
£1,550–2,175/$2,500–3,500

MARKS

Louis Tiffany's glass
companies used a
wide range of marks.
To avoid fakes, check
the mark carefully.
Etched signatures
for Favrile glass
include "L.C.T",
"L.C. Tiffany –
Favrile", "Louis C.
Tiffany – Favrile" or a
combination of these.

Bowls have been widely used over the centuries as luxury objects intended to display the skills of the glassmaker; only since the late 18thC have they been widely produced as functional tableware. Before the invention of free-blowing in the ancient Roman Empire, bowls were created by slumping – a technique developed in Mesopotamia as early as the 15thC BC in which a layer of hot glass was placed over a ceramic mould in a furnace or kiln and, as it cooled, assumed the shape of the mould. The finest examples, dating from about the 3rdC BC, include mosaic-glass bowls composed of fused pieces of multi-coloured glass canes, as well as bowls of "gold sandwich" glass – a decorative technique perfected in 18thC Bohemia as *Zwischengoldglas*, where gold leaf is placed between layers of clear glass. The invention of glass blowing in the 1stC AD revolutionized the production of bowls, as they could then be formed by blowing a gather to the desired shape, attaching a pontil iron, and expanding the paraison outwards. These bowls were often decorated with simple vertical ribbing, and strengthened with plain moulded feet. Similar wares were produced throughout the medieval period for the wealthy classes. In Venice the addition of a stem and foot to a shallow bowl transformed it into a tazza (see pp.122–7), used for ceremonial occasions and often richly enamelled. In the late 18thC the emergence of the complete glass table service led to the development of bowls for specialized uses, such as wine-glass coolers or rinsers, finger bowls and caddy bowls. Many larger, richly cut-engraved pieces were used for displaying flowers on a table.

EARLY BOWLS

Bowls made in and before the 18thC are extremely diverse in shape, style and decoration. Medieval examples of potash glass made in central Europe are generally small and slightly green-tinted, often with simple moulded decoration, though fine *filigrana* and *latticinio* items were produced in 16thC Venice. With the invention of lead glass, engraving and cutting were more popular methods of decoration in the 18thC and 19thC. Irish cut-glass pieces with distinctive boat, turnover rim or kettledrum shapes are particularly valuable and sought after.

▲ **MEDIEVAL GLASS**
The distinctive green tint of this rare, mould-blown small bowl or beaker, made in Germany or Bohemia *c.*1450, is characteristic of medieval central European glass. The precise purpose for which these bowls were made is unclear: they may have been drinking vessels or even storage containers. Like many medieval pieces, it bears traces of discoloration as a result of long burial in the ground. £1,000–1,500/$1,600–2,400

"LEMON-SQUEEZER" FEET
This unusual term describes a distinctive style of foot found on Irish Regency cut-glass bowls: they have a square base and high-domed cut shapes, moulded on the underside with ribbing to catch the light.

▶ IRISH CUT GLASS

Boat shapes are associated in particular with Irish cut-glass bowls from c.1780 to the 1830s. This bowl is typically cut with shallow diamonds and an ornate scalloped rim; however, the bobbin stem is quite unusual and adds to the value. While of good quality, aimed at the luxury market, these bowls can be irregular in shape. £2,000–3,000/ $3,200–4,800

◀ PUNCH-BOWL

In the early 18thC lead glass was still novel and very costly, so large items such as this engraved punch-bowl, dated 1720, would have been treasured and only used on special occasions. The elegant proportions and restrained decoration of a coat of arms are copied from silver punch-bowls of the same date. £3,000–5,000/$4,800–8,000

◀ WROCKWARDINE

This bottle-glass bowl (c.1800) with splattered white-glass decoration was produced at the Wrockwardine Wood factory in Shropshire. Pieces made by this factory are rare and collectable, but most English locally-produced glass for domestic use is quite common. £350–500/$560–800

▶ TURNOVER RIM

The turnover-rim-shaped bowl with a "lemon-squeezer" foot is another of the classic styles associated with Irish Regency cut glass. The rims are sometimes uneven because of the difficulty of manipulating hot glass into this form. Check for signs of wear on the base, as this is a good indication that the piece is genuine. £2,000–3,000/$3,200–4,800

LATER BOWLS

New developments in glass technology in the late 18thC and early 19thC meant that glass tableware was now affordable for a wider section of society. This, combined with the increasing refinement in etiquette at the dining and tea tables, resulted in the introduction of various types of bowls for specialized purposes. (The changes in eating habits and social customs today mean that these are now rarely used as originally intended.) Such bowls included wine glass coolers or rinsers (one for each diner), for washing or cooling drinking glasses between courses. These are less common from the mid-19thC, when it was more popular to have different styles of drinking glass used for the wines accompanying each course. Finger bowls filled with water were used for rinsing the fingers between courses. Glass caddy and sugar bowls were also employed in the preparation of tea – an often elaborate ritual.

◀ **GEORGIAN COOLER**
Early wine-glass coolers, like this 18thC example, generally have deeper bowls than their 19thC counterparts, as drinking glasses in this period had long stems and small bowls. The simple narrow fluting around the base of the bowl is also characteristic of Georgian pieces. £50–100/$80–160

▶ **POURING LIPS**
Wine glass coolers can be identified by the pouring lip on either side of the bowl, preventing the stem of the glass rolling around the rim. One lip is sufficient but most have two as that was quicker to fashion with a hot iron rod. This wide, engraved bowl is 19thC. £50–100/$80–160

◀ **18THC FINGER BOWL**
Finger bowls are similar in form to wine-glass coolers, but they do not have the pouring lips. This late 18thC bowl is engraved with a simple geometric band similar to that found on silver tableware of the period. These bowls can be a very affordable way of starting a collection of 18thC glass. £30–40/$50–65

CADDY BOWLS

In the 18thC and early 19thC tea was an expensive commodity, and it was kept locked away in tea caddies (generally silver containers placed in a wooden box) to prevent theft. Each box usually had two caddies – one for green tea and one for black – that sat either side of a glass bowl, called a caddy bowl. For many years it was thought that such bowls, now often separated from the box, were used for blending the tea, but today it is generally accepted that they were used for serving sugar. This caddy bowl, below, dates from c.1820. £50–100/$80–160

The elegant cut festoons are characteristic of the Neo-classical period.

Check for scratches inside the bowl caused by sugar crystals or spoons.

The tall, straight-sided shape with small rudimentary foot identifies this piece as a caddy bowl.

Most examples are of clear glass, but coloured pieces can also be found.

Check for chips and cracks around the rim and foot – the most vulnerable areas.

◀ THOMAS WEBB
After the repeal of the Excise Tax in 1845, English glassmakers returned to producing elaborately decorated large glass bowls. This richly cut piece (c.1928) in the "New York" pattern was made by the firm of Thomas Webb. Though similar to Webb pieces of the 19thC, the geometric elements echo 1920s Art Deco style. £700–900/$1,125–1,440

SUGAR BOWLS

19thC sugar bowls can be an interesting and affordable collecting area. They were made in a range of styles and colours, often in vividly-coloured late Victorian fancy glass, with ornate rims and handles.

Tazzas

Tazza – the Italian word for a cup – describes a type of wide, shallow or flat bowl or dish on a stemmed foot. The earliest examples were produced in 15thC Venice, and, like so much Venetian glassware, were probably inspired by Islamic footed glass bowls, with wide and hollow cylindrical stems, from Syria, and by similar engraved items made in silver. Venetian tazzas were luxury glassware, intended as wedding gifts – some feature enamelled portraits of a bride and groom in the centre – or for important ceremonies: many are depicted in contemporary paintings, and are sometimes shown as vessels for serving red wine. The finest pieces are decorated with enamel and gilding in the centre, sometimes with a coat of arms, and around the rim. Such items were copied much later in lead glass by 18thC English glassmakers, with elaborate stems following the style of drinking glasses. While still expensive, these may have been used not only for display – especially in a tiered pyramid arrangement of smaller tazzas on top of a larger one – but also for serving fruit and sweetmeats at the end of a meal, or by servants for presenting a glass of wine. During the 19thC tazzas, often also called comports, were produced in sets of varying sizes as dessert services, usually with matching sets of flat glass plates. Reasonably priced examples in both clear and coloured pressed glass were a speciality of US manufacturers, although more expensive pieces had high-quality cutting on the bowl and sometimes also the stem and foot. The more recent tazzas are still widely popular today as attractive serving dishes for cakes and fruit.

ENGLISH

Inspired by Venetian examples, tazzas were among the earliest types of glassware produced in England, from the early 18thC. They are thought to have been used as all-purpose serving dishes, or were stacked one on top of the other in decreasing sizes to create a centrepiece for a dining table or to display desserts and sweets – they would have been expensive decorative items affordable only by the rich. Like contemporary drinking glasses, most early and mid-18thC pieces are relatively plain: the shape was a shallow, sometimes flat dish on a stemmed foot, the style of which copied that on wine glasses.

▲ **BALUSTER STEM**
English tazzas made in the early 18thC feature two styles of stem: the baluster and the moulded-pedestal, or Silesian, stem. The former were made only until *c.*1730 and are much rarer, while the Silesian type, produced from *c.*1750, remained popular well into the 20thC. This low baluster tazza (*c.*1730) has a typically heavy knopped stem. Early pieces like this are smaller than later ones. £700–900/ $1,125–1,440

CONTINENTAL COPIES
As with early 18thC English drinking glasses, copies of baluster and Silesian-stemmed tazzas were made on the Continent. Made of soda glass, these are lighter in weight than English pieces, with hollow stems, and lack the distinctive grey tone of lead glass.

◀ PATCH STAND
This small tazza on a baluster stem with an upturned rim dates from *c.*1710 to *c.*1760 and is of a type often described as a patch stand – a little receptacle for holding the beauty spots applied to the face, which were fashionable in the 18thC. While this description might be accurate, there is only hearsay evidence for it. These tazzas make an interesting field in which to collect. Prices are usually in the range £200–300/$325–475.

▶ SALVER
This low tazza with a spreading foot (*c.*1720) is also called a salver. Such tazzas were made in many sizes, ranging in diameter from 15 to 45cm (6–18in), and were probably used for serving wine: at this time drinking glasses were not usually laid on the table, but filled on request by a servant. £300–500/$475–800

◀ 1840s STYLE
Silesian-stemmed tazzas were made in the 19thC as well as the 18thC, with few changes to the basic form, as seen in this example of *c.*1840s. The 19thC versions can often be identified by thicker stems, heavy weight and unevenly balanced shapes. Most tazzas of this form have folded feet, but in the 19thC the foot folds up. £300–400/$475–640

▶ CENTREPIECE
Examples like this Silesian-stemmed tazza from *c.*1750 were stacked in pyramid form to display confections of preserved and candied fruit, as well as "jelly" glasses for sweets, and patty pans with savoury delicacies at ball suppers. The form is much lighter and more refined than later, 19thC versions. £700–800/$1,125–1,275

LATER TAZZAS

In the 19thC the term "tazza" or "comport" was used in a much broader sense to describe any type of stemmed glass dish or bowl for serving a variety of delicacies at the dinner or tea table, or simply for display. While some flat-topped tazzas in the 18thC style were still produced in the 19thC, they were generally made by mechanical press-moulding rather than by the much more expensive and laborious method of hand "spinning" previously used to make crown glass for window panes. Whereas 18thC tazzas were generally made in clear glass, later versions are found in a great variety of colours and decoration, from cutting and engraving to *latticinio* and enamelling – some of the most expensive items, especially those by French glassmakers, also have elaborate figural handles. Sets of tazzas of different sizes, used for serving fruit, desserts or cakes, were also popular as expensive wedding gifts during the second half of the 19thC.

BACCARAT TAZZA

Vases and tazzas in opaline glass are among the most characteristic of Baccarat's products. Opaline glass was made by adding gold oxide to the batch to create a richly translucent body, often coloured with other metallic oxides. This rare tazza (*c.*1830), with ormolu handles, combines an amethyst-glass bowl with a border of *boule de savon* ("soap-bubble") glass, so called because of the rainbow hues visible when it catches the light. £4,000–4,500/ $6,400–7,200

◀ **DESSERT TAZZA**
Victorian tazzas were often made in sets of two or three of different sizes as part of a large glass dessert service – but individual pieces rather than complete sets are more usually found today. However, single tazzas are still popular with glass enthusiasts as they are very useful pieces for serving fruits, chocolates and cakes. This example with all-over cutting dates from *c.*1860; similar designs were made by press-moulding, and these can be distinguished by visible mould lines and a slightly glossy, opaque surface. £100–150/$160–240

▶ **SCOTTISH**
LATTICINIO

This *latticinio* tazza (*c*.1870),
part of a dessert service made
by Alexander Jenkinson at the
Norton Park Glassworks, is a
rare example of Scottish-made
Venetian Revival glass. Tazzas
inspired by Venetian styles
were also made in France in
the mid-19thC (see below), but
the coloured-glass twists in this
Scottish piece are much more
uneven than in French examples.
£500–700/$800–1,125

**19THC *LATTICINIO*
& THE VENETIAN
ORIGINALS**

19thC *latticinio* wares
can be distinguished
from the Venetian
originals by the use
of lead rather than
soda glass, by the greater
complexity of decoration,
and by the much wider
range of colours.

◀ **ST LOUIS**
LATTICINIO

This small tazza, like
similar 18thC examples, is
described as a patch stand, but
by the time it was made in
c.1850 the fashion for beauty
spots or patches had long
since died out, so it is more
likely that it was intended as a
"cabinet" piece to be admired

alongside other pieces of high-
quality decorative glass. The
fine white *latticinio* decoration,
inspired by 17thC Venetian
glass, is typical of ornamental
glass made by the French
factory of St Louis. Other
19thC St Louis vases and
tazzas feature white threads
combined with pink or blue.
£400–500/$640–800

▶ **CRYSTAL TAZZA**

Fine glass tazzas were
still made in the early
20thC as display pieces: this fine
Art Deco crystal tazza (*c*.1925)
by the Italian firm of Vetri di
Arte, signed "VEDAR" with a
Roman numeral, is enamelled
with a Classically-inspired design
of dancing women. Art Deco
pieces like this are very rare.
£800–1,200/$1,275–1,925

VENETIAN & AMERICAN

The glass tazza is a form particularly associated with Venetian glassware, and some of the finest surviving examples were made in Venice from the 15thC to the 18thC. Unlike later examples these nearly always have distinctive low, hollow, spreading feet and shallow bowls with upturned lips or rims, inspired by contemporary examples in silver. Most are made of clear glass with enamelled and gilded decoration, usually the coat of arms of the owner, allegorical scenes or formal diaper patterns. Such tazzas were made for the wealthy, and, although their precise function is unknown, they were used only on special occasions, such as weddings, probably as a show of wealth, and so are exceptionally valuable and prized by collectors today. By contrast, American tazzas were made only from the 19thC: most are made of pressed glass, either plain or in a range of colours, but some good-quality pieces feature cut and engraved decoration.

◀ THE LION OF ST MARK
An early Venetian tazza (*c*.1500), this example is typically enamelled in the centre in yellow, blue and green with a lion standing on a mound beneath the sun: this may refer to the lion of St Mark, the symbol of Venice, which suggests that the tazza could possibly have been used at important state functions held in the city.
£3,000–5,000/$4,800–8,000

▶ ISLAMIC INSPIRATION
This early 16thC gilded and enamelled tazza features mould-blown ribbing around the bowl and is unusually ornate. As with many early Venetian wares, the geometric pattern around the rim is inspired by Islamic glass. Copies of early tazzas were made but can be identified by their heavier weight (they were made of lead glass rather than the original soda glass) and more uniform shape; the coats of arms are mostly fictitious.
£7,000–9,000/$11,200–14,400

◀ LAVISH DECORATION

Heavily decorated Venetian tazzas in pristine condition, like this early 16thC enamelled example, will always fetch higher prices than plainer ones. This piece is gilded, and enamelled in the centre with a stylized flowerhead, while the underside of the rim is embellished with a gilt scale-pattern band enriched with coloured enamel dots.
£12,000–15,000/$19,200–24,000

▶ CUT AND ENGRAVED DECORATION

This pair of tazzas, made by the firm of Thomas G. Hawkes of Corning, New York, c.1890, features the high-quality cut and engraved decoration that was a trademark of luxury tableware from this firm. This combination of decorative techniques is rarely found on European wares. Less expensive imitations would have been made by press-moulding.
£1,000–2,000/$1,600–3,200

◀ "CHANDELIER" PATTERN

From the early 19thC, Pittsburgh, Pennsylvania, became renowned for its high-quality cut lead glass in the English style, culminating in the complex all-over "brilliant-cut" styles, combining various patterns such as hobnail, star and strawberry diamond. The style was widely copied by pressed-glass makers in the USA and Europe. This "Chandelier" pattern cake stand was produced c.1880 in Pittsburgh.
£95–150/$150–250

Pressed Glass

The development of pressed glass was perhaps the most revolutionary event in glass technology in the 19thC, enabling high-volume production of inexpensive glassware such as plates, cups, mugs, drinking glasses and cake stands. While fashioning glassware by blowing molten glass into a shaped mould was known from Roman times, and decanter stoppers and rummer bases had been produced by using small hand-operated presses in the 18thC, it was not until the 1820s in the USA that mechanized production of glassware was introduced. The technique of pressing glass involved pouring a measured quantity of hot glass into a metal hinged mould (often in several parts), then lowering a plunger to force the glass into all parts of the mould, and as the glass cooled it retained the shape of the mould on one side and that of the plunger on the other; from c.1870 the advent of "fire-polishing" – which involved placing the object in a furnace – enabled the ridges left by the mould to be removed. The invention of the steam-powered press in the early 1860s increased the rate at which mould-pressed items could be manufactured, and further reduced costs. At first the technique was used to produce copies of heavily cut glass, but gradually distinctive pressed-glass styles emerged. Early press-moulded wares are particularly associated with US glassmakers, especially the Boston & Sandwich Glass Co., the New England Glass Co. and the Mount Washington Glass Co., all in Massachusetts, but production soon spread to the emerging Midwest factories, and to factories in Europe.

ENGLISH & EUROPEAN

The technique of pressing glass was introduced into Britain and continental Europe from the USA in the late 1830s. English firms were among the most prolific pressed-glass manufacturers – in the early 19thC most were based in the Midlands. Production expanded in the 1850s, as the Excise Tax on the weight of raw materials in glassmaking was finally abolished in 1845. From this period the leading producers were in the north, for example Molineaux, Webb & Co. of Manchester, Henry Greener & Co. of Sunderland, and John Sowerby's Ellison Glassworks and George Davidson & Co., both of Gateshead.

◀ **MALACHITE DOG**
Animals, such as this small late 19thC model of a dog, were among the most popular subjects for pressed-glass figures. This piece is made in a marbled glass often called "malachite" as it imitates the veining of the stone. As it is unmarked, it will be worth less than a marked item.
£100–150/$160–240

▶ **NURSERY RHYMES**
This late 19thC "opal" vase, with the firm's mark and a pattern number, from John Sowerby's Ellison Glassworks, is decorated with a nursery rhyme theme, inspired by the book illustration of Walter Crane. Such pieces are among the most collectable pressed glass today.
£180–220/$290–350

◀ MULTIPLICATION
This Sowerby "opal" cylindrical vase is similar in style to the nursery rhyme example shown below left. This piece is moulded in relief with a scene relating to "Multiplication". £180–220/$290–350

▼ THREE SWANS
Sowerby was among the firms that experimented with coloured glass from the 1870s. Its cream-coloured "Patent Ivory Queen's Ware", as seen in this vase with a pattern of three swans, was a successful result. The sharp delineation of the decoration adds to the value. £200–300/$325–475

ENGLISH PRESSED GLASS
As well as tableware, English pressed-glass firms also produced ornamental figures, and items commemorating important national events, e.g. Queen Victoria's golden and diamond jubilees. Many items were made in the style of more expensive cut glass.

▼ "CRYSTAL" PLATE
The decoration of this pressed-glass "crystal" plate, made by the French firm of St Louis c.1870, imitates both the lacy style of American pressed glass and, in the centre, cut glass. Plates, perhaps because of their simple form, were among the most commonly produced pressed-glass products, and can still be found at reasonable prices today. £30–50/$50–80

▲ SMALL SOUVENIR
This small brown cauldron-shaped vase by Henry Greener & Co. of Sunderland illustrates the marbled effect that many pressed-glass manufacturers tried to create. These small pieces were often souvenirs brought home from a day trip away and are still quite widely available today. As moulds were expensive to cut, such pieces were commonly made over long periods and in many styles and colours. £60–80/$100–130

AMERICAN

Press-moulded glass, an American invention, revolutionized the production of glass worldwide, making affordable glassware available to the masses for the first time. It is not certain who first invented it, but this method was employed for small tableware by the late 1820s at the New England Glass Co. and the Boston & Sandwich Glass Co., both in Massachusetts. The technique came into widespread use from the 1830s and spread to Europe, and, especially after the introduction of the steam-driven mechanized press in the 1860s, was employed for most glass tableware and domesticware made in the USA. Pressed glass was produced in an huge range of named patterns and colours owing to the rivalry that developed between manufacturers. One of the most sought-after types was the "lacy glass" developed c.1830 by Deming Jarves of the Boston & Sandwich Glass Co.

RARE INKSTAND

Inkstands, consisting of a penholder and two receptacles for holding ink and pounce (fine sand for drying ink), were made in glass from the 18thC. This exceptionally rare and valuable pressed-glass inkstand (c.1830) by the Boston & Sandwich Glass Co. is one of the earliest surviving pieces of American pressed glass, and one of only about six known examples. £15,600–20,000/$25,000–32,000

▼ ELABORATE SALT This ornate salt container, produced by the Boston & Sandwich Glass Co. c.1830–40, features the scrolls and flowers characteristic of some of the over-elaborate wares made in the Victorian era. Clear-glass versions such as this are less expensive – sometimes about a quarter of the price – than pieces made in green, blue and other colours today. The Boston & Sandwich Glass Co. was the USA's leading maker of pressed glass. £50–75/$80–125

◀ MONKEYS Small mugs are typical of the inexpensive tableware made in pressed glass, sold as ornaments and for everyday use. This "monkey" pattern mug, made in the 1880s in Pittsburgh, is in a rare amethyst-coloured non lead glass (they are more commonly found in clear and opalescent glass). On early mugs the handles were made separately, but later models were modelled as one piece. £65–95/$100–150

▶ **"JUMBO" RACK**
Spoon racks and
holders, a uniquely
American type of
tableware, were made
in pressed glass in many
styles throughout the
19thC. This "Jumbo"
pattern spoon rack,
made in Carlton, Ohio,
in 1884, commemorates
P. T. Barnum's famous
elephant Jumbo. It is
a good example of the
type of pressed glass
produced by the new
factories in the Midwest.
£325–450/$500–700

▲ **BANANA STAND**
This stand, made in the
"King's Crown" pattern
in Pittsburgh in the
1890s and inspired by
the art glass of the time,
combines a clear-glass
body with a stained ruby
rim and sharply defined
pattern. It is not certain
whether such elaborate
pieces were used for
serving fruit
or intended for
displaying glass
fruit on a dining
table. £450–
550/$700–900

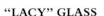

"LACY" GLASS
This pressed glass, made to look like
real lace, has decorative patterns of
moulded foliage, flowers, scrolls or
rosettes on a stippled background.
It was used mainly on cups and plates,
but also on jugs, bowls and trays.

◀ **AMERICAN
INFLUENCE**
The production of
colourful and useful
pressed-glass wares spread
from the US to Europe
in the 19thC: this
decorative pickle vase
(c.1890) was made by
the English firm of John
Derbyshire & Co. of
Salford. Derbyshire wares
are generally signed with
the company mark –
the initials "JD" and an
anchor. £60–90/$100–150

Matching glass table services were produced from the late 18thC, principally to compete with those in porcelain and cream-coloured earthenware. The greater demand for glassware for the dining and tea tables was due mainly to the ever-increasing refinement of dining etiquette, especially among the aspirational Victorian middle classes, which required specialized utensils for each aspect of eating and drinking. Not only were larger items such as decanters and tazzas decorated to match, but also the varying shapes of drinking glasses and a huge array of smaller items, such as wine-glass coolers, salt cellars, pickle jars and finger bowls. Glassware was also made for serving punch, the proper mixing of which was seen as an essential requirement for the fashionable gentleman; while punch-bowls were generally made of silver, glass was used for small drinking vessels and the decanter-shaped serving implement known as a toddy lifter. Some tableware was, however, rarely made in glass before the 20thC – such as glass tea cups – while before the invention of pressed glass in the 1830s glass dinner plates were rare. Other wares, such as patty pans, originally made in glass have been superseded by cheaper metalware. Small glass tableware is one of the most intriguing and stimulating areas in which to collect today as there is such a large variety of items available – most items are also quite modestly priced and so can be particularly appealing to the novice collector.

ENGLISH & IRISH

England and Ireland led the way in the development of specialized glass items for the dining table, perhaps because their renowned lead glass is more durable and robust than the Continental soda and potash glass. The most collectable items today are those made in the late 18thC and early 19thC, which are often decorated with simple-cut patterns; pressed-glass tableware made from the mid-19thC onwards is more accessible but less valuable.

▲ TRENCHER SALTS
At 18thC and 19thC tables each diner would have had a small salt cellar, often called a trencher salt. These were usually made in sets, like these opaque-white glass salts (c.1760) embellished with moulded fluting and enamelled flower sprays. The decoration on these salts will increase their value considerably, as many salts are plain and functional. £1,000–2,000/$1,600–3,200 (for the pair)

◀ BUTTER DISH
Glass butter dishes were popular from the end of the 18thC until c.1850. This example of c.1820 is decorated with simple bands of horizontal and vertical cutting. These dishes nearly always have stands – perhaps for ice to keep the butter cool. £400–500/$650–800

▶ THE TODDY LIFTER

The toddy lifter – a hollow glass vessel used for transferring punch from the bowl to the drinking glass – enjoyed a limited period of popularity from c.1810 to c.1830 in England and Ireland. Shaped like a miniature decanter, with a capacity of a single wine glass, it has holes in both top and bottom and is used like a pipette – the bulbous base is dipped into the punch to collect the liquid; a vacuum is created by placing the thumb over the top hole, ensuring that no liquid leaks out. The punch is released into the glass by opening the hole again. This example dates from c.1820. £100–150/ $160–240

Check carefully for cracks or chips around the top and bottom holes, as these areas are particularly prone to damage.

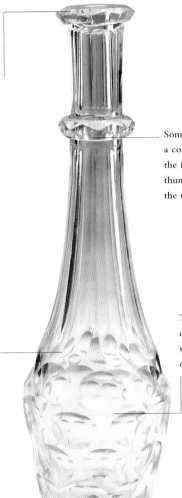

Some pieces have a collar as a grip for the fingers when the thumb is placed over the top hole.

The body is usually decorated with simple cutting or optical moulding.

The body should have a distinctive grey tone characteristic of English and Irish lead glass.

◀ MILK LADLE

Oddly named a piggin, this item was used for ladling milk. Piggins were popular, especially in Ireland, around 1800. This 1830s example, decorated with cutting imitating the staves of a barrel, would have been used in a wealthy household. £100–150/$160–240

▶ SERVING PLATE

Glass plates were rare before the advent of pressed glass. Like most early plates, this Irish one (c.1820) has simple star-cutting under the centre and a low flat decorated rim. It would have been used for fruit or dessert. £200–300/$325–475

AMERICAN

The earliest American settlers imported European glass tableware, but from the late 18thC, enamelled, cut and engraved, mainly colourless, tableware was produced at the factory of Henry William Stiegel at Manheim, Pennsylvania, and the New Bremen glassworks of John Frederick Amelung in Frederick County, Maryland. However, the popularity of mould-blown glass and the 1820s invention of pressed glass led to the widespread mass production of inexpensive tableware for the domestic market – most was similar to that found in Europe, but some distinctively American forms emerged, such as the exotic banana stand, the spoon rack and cup plates used to hold handleless cups while tea or coffee cooled in and was drunk from the saucer. Complete table services and domesticware were available in a huge range of named patterns and patented colours.

▶ "BELLFLOWER" PATTERN

The Boston & Sandwich Glass Co. produced this "Bellflower" pattern covered sweetmeat dish with pedestal foot in the 1850s. This example is made in Flint (lead) glass; the same design was later made in non-Flint glass by the McKee Brothers and others. The pattern was very collectable, and there were several variations made, mostly in clear glass but on rare occasions in different colours. Flint glass raises higher prices than non-Flint. £250–375/$400–600

▼ "CHOCOLATE" GLASS

This late 19thC pressed-glass butter dish is made of "chocolate" glass, invented by the Indiana Tumbler and Goblet Co., also known for its "Holly Amber" glass. This style is known as the "Dewey" pattern and is much sought after. Unlike earlier clear-glass English butter dishes, this piece does not have a stand below the dish. £95–150/$150–250

◀ BOAR'S HEAD

Milk glass is opaque-white glass created by adding tin oxide to the batch. Inspired by Venetian *lattimo* glass, used from the 15thC to make beakers and cups, it was revived in the late 19thC and remained popular until World War I. This covered dish in the shape of a boar's head was made c.1880s. Domestic and table wares in animal shapes made before World War I are popular with collectors today and have been widely copied. £625–950/$1,000–1,500

◀ TIFFANY FAVRILE SALTS

In wealthy households, small salt cellars were provided for each diner, as seen in this set of twelve salts in Favrile glass by Tiffany (*c.*1900). Favrile, patented in 1894 by Tiffany, is a glass treated with metallic oxides to create a shimmering iridescent surface, similar to that found on ancient Roman glass, which is caused by long burial. Most of this glass was used for decorative items such as vases, so useful wares like salts are very collectable – more so if they are in their original case. £3,750–5,000/$6,000–8,000 (the set)

CUP PLATES

These are among the most collectable pieces of early pressed-glass American tableware. They are found in both clear and coloured glass and were produced from the 1830s. Examples with commemorative designs or patriotic emblems, such as eagles, are particularly rare and therefore highly valuable.

▶ ROSEWATER DISPENSER

Wares made by the firm of Louis Comfort Tiffany (1848–1933), probably the most celebrated American glassmaker, are highly prized by collectors of glass and of Art Nouveau design today. This rare, sinuous plant-like rosewater dispenser (*c.*1900) in Favrile glass (see above) was originally used to refresh the hands between courses, but most likely became a purely decorative piece. It is based on 18th and 19thC Islamic designs. £15,500–22,000/$25,000–35,000

◀ "MARY GREGORY" GLASS

This coloured-glass oblong plate, decorated in white enamel with a scene of children at play, is a type of glass known as "Mary Gregory", possibly named after an employee at the Boston & Sandwich Glass Co. in Sandwich, Massachusetts. Wares in this style are made in cranberry, dark green and amethyst, as well as yellow. £100–200/$160–325

CANDLESTICKS & CANDELABRA

Candlesticks were made in the medieval period, but only with the invention of brilliant, clear lead glass was glass more widely used for lighting. The patterns of early lead-glass candlesticks and later candelabra and hanging chandeliers were copied from brass and silver models, with elegant, plain knopped baluster stems. Throughout the 18thC English candlesticks featured stems with decoration following that of contemporary drinking glasses, such as air and opaque twists and moulded-pedestal designs. Candelabra were produced from the mid-18thC and are similar in design to candlesticks, but have two or more removable branches to which the sconces (candle holders) and drip pans for collecting molten wax are attached. In the 19thC they were often embellished with lustres – cut-glass drops or rods hung from the sconce to increase the volume of light reflected. Chandeliers are the most impressive and costly form of glass lighting.

▶ RARE 17THC GLASS PIECE

Glass candlesticks pre-dating 1700 are extremely scarce and valuable. This *façon de Venise* candlestick, made in The Netherlands in the 17thC, is typically decorated with diamond-point engraved foliate scrolls. The high-domed foot and inverted baluster stem are copied directly from silver candlesticks. This piece is surprisingly light to handle as it is made of soda glass.
£8,000–12,000/$12,800–19,200

▼ AIR-TWIST STEM

This rare English candlestick (*c.*1750) with an air-twist stem has a moulded domed foot (for stability) and a rib-moulded sconce, with decorative beaded knops at the top and bottom of the stem. Candlesticks with all the varieties of 18thC stems on wine glasses can be found today. However, they may be more difficult to date than wine glasses as each style covers a wide period.
£2,500–3,500/$4,000–5,600

◀ TAPERSTICK

This candlestick with a faceted stem is a taperstick – a smaller kind of stick for holding a taper, or thin candle, which was used for lighting tobacco pipes or melting sealing wax. Tapersticks are generally 10–13cm/4–5in in height, about half the size of a normal candlestick, and were made singly rather than as a pair. Faceted candlesticks continued to be made in the 19thC so dating can be problematic.
£425–525/$675–850

▶ ARGAND LAMP

As well as candlesticks, candelabra and chandeliers, glass was also an ideal medium for lamp covers or shades, as it protected the candle or wick from the elements without reducing the amount of light emitted. This elegant Regency hanging oil lamp, with a cut glass base and vase-shaped gilt-bronze finial, is known as an Argand lamp – a type producing a bright flame invented by Aimé Argand in Switzerland in 1784. Very costly when first produced, these lamps retain their value today if complete with their original parts. £30,000–40,000/$48,000–64,000

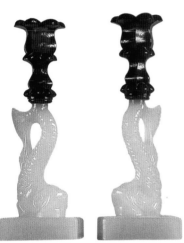

◀ NOVELTY DESIGNS

Most candlesticks were made in pairs, to maximize the light, and pairs are usually worth more than twice the value of a single item. This pair (*c.*1850), with opaque-white dolphin-shaped stems, was made by the Boston & Sandwich Glass Co. Figural and naturalistic designs became popular in the 19thC, reflecting a taste for novelty styles. £1,250–2,500/$2,000–4,000 (the pair)

REGENCY CHANDELIERS

Chandeliers made in the Regency period (1811–20) are perhaps the most familiar type today. A wide metal hoop incorporates the candle sockets, with the central stem and base hidden by glittering festoons or chains of small faceted cut-glass drops. These were affordable only to the wealthiest households because of the very high costs of hand-cutting each drop or pendant.

◀ COLOURED GLASS

During the 19thC, candelabra became ever more elaborate, with numerous branches and candle holders ornamented with lustres. Coloured glass – especially red, as in this mid-19thC Bohemian example – was very popular, principally for its decorative value as it did not reflect as much light as clear glass. Spears, crescents or pineapples often embellish the top of the stem. Always check very carefully for missing branches (indicated by holes in a brass plate at the top of the stem), lustres and shades, and that all parts match in colour and style of decoration. £10,000–15,000/$16,000–24,000

BOTTLES

Bottles were among the first functional items made in glass for the purpose of storing and transporting perfumes, oils and wine. From the 1stC AD the principal method of bottle manufacture was free-blowing, particularly suitable for this type of glassware since one of the most straightforward shapes that can be produced by expanding a gather of a molten glass is a vessel with a narrow neck. The earliest complete examples surviving in any number date from the mid-17thC, particularly those from England, where a distinctive dark-green, almost black, bottle glass was developed. These practical vessels, which were exported on a large scale to continental Europe, feature bulbous bodies with tapering necks, and kicks, or indentations, in the bases. This design was later replaced by more globular shapes and, by the late 18thC, by the tall narrow form that is most familiar in bottles manufactured today.

◀ CORAL COATING

This intriguing bottle (*c.*1740) covered with coral was found by divers off Bermuda, and may have been dropped overboard from a ship or formed part of the cargo of a wreck. Dutch bottles of this date are fairly common in the West Indies and in Surinam, as they were used as ballast but discarded before the return voyage. It is difficult to remove the build-up of coral, and unwise, as this will probably damage the bottle. £200–300/$325–475

▶ RARE SERVING BOTTLE

Bottles dating from the mid-17thC often have applied rings around the neck, used to attach stoppers. This rare blue-tinted Dutch serving bottle has a pewter cap and mount to stop the contents spilling. The neck ring would have strengthened the body. Most English bottles of this date were free-blown, but the decoration on the body of this bottle would have been produced by blowing the gather into a mould. £7,000–9,000/$11,200–14,400

▲ SHAFT AND GLOBE

All bottles dating from the mid-17thC are especially rare, and if in good condition can command high prices, since most were discarded. The "shaft-and-globe" shape (*c.*1660) can also be found in ceramic and leather bottles of the period. The irregular shape indicates that the bottle was free-blown – later examples were mould-blown for ease of stacking and to standardize capacity. £8,000–10,000/$12,800–16,000

◀ COLLEGE BOTTLE

Bottles such as this one (*c*.1780), with a seal "ASCR" representing All Souls' Common Room, would have been used for serving wine to university students at the various Oxford colleges. It was found, like many 18thC bottles, in the cellars of All Souls' College in the late 1960s. These bottles are fairly common. The straight cylindrical shape and relatively short neck date it to the late 18thC. £150–250/ $240–400

SEAL BOTTLES

In the 18thC wine bottles were filled directly by the wine merchant from his barrels, so the owner identified his bottles by impressing a seal with a coat of arms or initials, and sometimes a date, onto a blob of molten glass applied to the body. Seals of taverns and colleges can be found as well as those of individuals.

◀ BRISTOL CRUET BOTTLE

Cruets for oil, vinegar and other condiments were introduced to England from France in the late 17thC and usually comprised a silver frame with silver castors and glass bottles. This Bristol glass cruet bottle would have been used for "kyan" or cayenne pepper and is similar in style to the Bristol-glass decanters produced in the late 18thC and early 19thC. Always check on such items that the gilding has not been worn through over-handling. £250–350/$400–560

◀ ART NOUVEAU STYLE

Perfume bottles were part of the range of high-quality luxury art glass created by the Tiffany Glass & Decorating Co. at the turn of the 20thC. This silver-mounted example (*c*.1900) has the undulating and twisting shape and decoration characteristic of Art Nouveau style. The body of the bottle is made of iridescent Tiffany Favrile glass. £9,500–12,500/$15,000–20,000

The inter-war and post-war years were a period of social change, and designers, manufacturers and public alike were eager for new styles.

In 1925 the *Exposition des Arts Decoratifs et Industrielles Modernes* in Paris launched the Art Deco style, ideally suited to the luxury glass produced by French designers and manufacturers such as Emile Gallé, and René Lalique, and the Tiffany Studios and Steuben Glassworks in the USA. Meanwhile in Scandinavia a more democratic approach to new glass was emerging, led by the Finns Alvar and Aino Aalto, who were designing elegant and functional tableware in a new Modernist style. In Sweden designers and manufacturers such as Orrefors and Kosta were making both affordable tableware and a range of engraved glass that was shown at the Stockholm Exhibition of 1930, and toured Britain in 1931, where it influenced leading designers. In Austria the designer/architects of the Wiener Werkstatte also experimented with new forms.

The Organic Design in Home Furniture Exhibition, held in New York in 1940, was the showcase for the fluid shapes that became known as the New Look. In the 1940s and 1950s it was Scandinavians and Italians who interpreted it most successfully, with Nils Landberg's work for Orrefors, Per Lutken's designs for the Danish Holmegaards Glassworks, Tapio Wirkkala at Ittala in Finland, and a range of lively coloured glass from Italian manufacturers. In the 1960s the American studio-glass movement encouraged a flowering of talent.

INTER-WAR YEARS

Many English glassmakers were slow to change and looked back to the historical styles of the 19thC, but some established firms made a range of luxury cut glass to compete with the inexpensive glassware flooding in from Czechoslovakia. New companies sprang up which concentrated on cased and coloured glass, such as Monart and Gray-Stan. In the USA, luxury glass made for the top end of the market was matched, in the Depression years, by vast quantities of very cheap mechanically mass-produced glass.

◀ **GRAY-STAN BOWL**
This Venetian-style fruit bowl was made by the small English glasshouse Gray-Stan (1926–36), makers of transparent coloured glass and pastel-shaded coloured and cased glass. Pieces with "Gray-Stan" engraved on them or the Gray-Stan mark on the base are especially sought after.
£400–500/$640–800

▲ **ELNE VASE**
Orrefors' success led to many imitations. This vase was made by Elne, a Swedish factory, in the early 1930s. It is well made, although nowhere near as valuable as an Orrefors original, but preferable to the Orrefors copies still being made in eastern Europe.
£200–300/$325–475

HARRY POWELL

Harry Powell joined the English glass house
Whitefriars in 1873 when it was still known
as James Powell & Sons of London, and was
responsible for the majority of the company's
glass designs until his retirement in 1919.
His passion for historical glass and fascination
with the natural world are clearly shown in
this goblet. Designed primarily for display,
probably before 1919, the goblet remained
in production until the mid-1930s.
£2,000–3,000/$3,200–4,800

• The stylized engraved irises on the bowl
of the glass reflect Harry Powell's interest
in the natural world and are influenced by
the organic Art Nouveau style of the late
19thC and early 20thC.

• The colour in the twisted stem is produced
by the inclusion of gold foil.

• The folded foot pictured here was
characteristically used on early 18thC
glasses; from c.1740 a flat foot was more
commonly used.

• Similar goblets can be found in coloured
glass, with ribbed or plain bowls; engraved
examples, such as this one, are rare and
therefore more valuable.

◀ **LEAF PATTERN**
W. Clyne Farquharson
produced a range of
outstanding designs for
John Walsh Walsh from
the mid-1930s to 1951.
One of his most popular
designs was the engraved
Leaf pattern, launched in
1936 and used on large
bowls, vases, decanters,
jugs and tumblers.
Pieces are signed
Clyne Farquharson
in diamond point on
the base. £700–900/
$1,125–1,440

▼ **DEPRESSION GLASS**
Many US glassmakers
survived the 1930s by
producing automatically-
pressed glass at prices to
tempt even the very
poorest. Huge amounts
of matching cheap

tableware was produced
that is now eagerly
collected for its historical
value and contemporary
look. As with any
inexpensive pieces, good
condition is essential.
£15–25/$25–40

ART DECO

The *Exposition des Arts Decoratifs et Industrielles Modernes* in Paris in 1925 was both the showcase for the new style and the origin of its name. At the top end of the market, French glassmakers in particular used angular forms, geometric enamelled decoration and dramatic colour combinations; Scandinavian designers focused on a typically Art Deco contrast of clear and black glass, often engraved with highly stylized motifs that in turn strongly influenced such leading designers as Keith Murray in Britain, while in Austria, Josef Hoffmann's faceted monochromatic designs led the trend towards chunky forms. These stylistic elements were adapted and incorporated into a huge range of tableware, of varying quality, especially the decanters, cocktail shakers and drinking glasses that flooded onto the market as manufacturers sought to capitalize on the new hedonistic lifestyle that Art Deco epitomized.

◀ FRENCH TANTALUS

The tantalus – a locking frame for decanters – was essentially a late 19thC phenomenon, and the rare Art Deco examples were luxury items, often made for millionaires' yachts or the newly fashionable ocean-going liners. The superb quality of this French example is evident in the well-made frame veneered in burr walnut, the cut-glass decanters with silver mounts and the original matching glasses, all of which are present. £2,000–3,000/ $3,200–4,800

▶ FRENCH DUCK DECANTER

Novelty items such as this duck decanter and glasses are very popular with collectors. Because they are highly sought after and valuable, copies are being made, and original mounts are sometimes fitted with new glass. £700–900/$1,125–1,440

◀ BOHEMIAN PIECE

This mould-blown decanter, cut, etched, engraved and enamelled, is quintessentially Art Deco. Typically, such pieces were made in Bohemia, where glassmakers produced quantities of tableware imitating French designs. £300–500/$475–800

GATE VASE

The Stockholm Exhibition of 1930 illustrated the skill of Swedish designer Simon Gate (1883–1945), who designed tableware, engraved glass and cut-glass vases that exploited the optical qualities of clear glass. This large mould-blown Orrefors vase, with its Art Deco black foot, was designed and signed by Gate for the Exhibition and is more a rare work of art than functional. £1,000–1,250/$1,600–2,000

DRINKING GLASSES

Comparatively few glasses have survived, although produced in quantity. Look for examples with a strong Art Deco feel and in excellent condition.

◀ PART OF A SET

Most decanters were accompanied by sets of six glasses. Few sets have survived intact, and individual glasses, especially stylish ones like this example, are a good and inexpensive starting point for Art Deco collectors, who may over time be able to build up a set. £30–50/$50–80

▲ COCKTAIL GLASS

During the Jazz Age drinking became socially acceptable, and cocktail shakers and glasses were produced in large quantities throughout Europe. Like many Art Deco cocktail glasses, this mould-blown and cut Bohemian example, with its practical wide flared rim, relies on dramatic shape and colour for appeal rather than the intricate ornate decoration which had been used on earlier glasses. £30–50/$50–80

◀ DECORATIVE BUT IMPRACTICAL

This striking Bohemian glass is, like many Art Deco tumblers, essentially a small and supremely decorative sculpture rather than a practical piece of tableware. Although the heavy base makes it stable, it holds very little, and its chunky form makes it difficult to drink out of. Any damage that detracts from its visual appeal will reduce its value, so check for chips to the rim or damage to the enamelling. £30–50/$50–80

POST-WAR DESIGN

Just as the Art Deco style had offered a new beginning after World War I, so too new stylistic movements offered relief from the austerity of the early post-war years. In the 1940s and 1950s, Scandinavian designers experimented with the organic shapes of the New Look as well as continuing the tradition of restrained minimalist lines; in Italy stylish, exuberant and colourful glass was produced by the leading Venetian glass houses. British glassmakers were initially slow to respond to the New Look, but came to the fore with the studio-glass movement that had begun in the USA in the 1960s. Scandinavian and Italian glass, especially by well-known designers, is an established collecting area. Early inexpensive post-war domestic glass by less illustrious makers is just beginning to be collected and can still be reasonably priced; the sculptural pieces by well-known makers are far more expensive but may well prove to be the "antiques" of tomorrow.

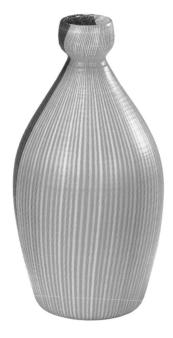

◀ VENINI *TESSUTO* VASE

The Venini glassworks (est. 1921) was one of the major Italian glassworks, celebrated for its bold use of colour and original forms and decorative techniques, as seen in this *tessuto* vase – named after its fabric-like decoration – designed by Carlo Scarpa. It is marked, with an acid stamp, "Venini Murano Italia".
£1,500–2,500/$2,400–4,000

▶ DRUNKEN BRICKLAYER

Made from 1967 to *c.*1977, the Whitefriars "Drunken Bricklayer" vase, designed by Geoffrey Baxter, came in two sizes and several colours, including this blue. These vases usually fetch from £75–85/$125–135 but this piece is far more valuable because it is a rare, possibly unique, example in which the "drunken" central block leans out from the other two. £400–600/$640–950

▼ SPLIT TRIANGLE

Colin Reid is one of the new generation of British studio-glass artists. This kiln-formed mould-cast piece reflects a preoccupation with split elements – "I like things that fit together", Reid says. The price his pieces command confirms that they are seen as original and unique works of art rather than domestic wares. £4,000–6,000/$6,400–9,600

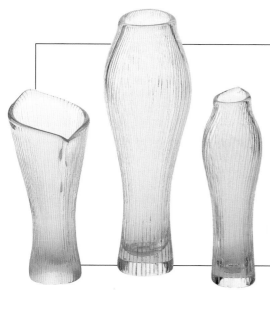

TAPIO WIRKKALA VASES

The versatile Finnish designer Tapio Wirkkala (1915–85) was at the forefront of glass design in the early post-war years. In 1946 he joined the Ittala glassworks, for which he designed a range of internationally recognized glass that included elegant domestic pieces as well as sculptural art glass. His love of the Finnish landscape inspired the textured, frosted, ice-like finishes seen on much of his clear colourless glass. The group of vases shown here was made by Ittala in the late 1940s and is a classic example of his use of organic shapes and textured surfaces. £150–250/$240–400 (each)

▲ VENINI PAPERWEIGHT

This glass fish is a good example of quirky design, and is one of several similar decorative fish made and signed by the Venini glassworks in the early 1960s that show off the company's mastery of form and colour. Such novelty pieces are highly popular in their own right as well as offering an affordable entrée into collecting glass by a major Italian manufacturer. £300–500/$475–800

▶ DALE CHIHULY VASES

One of the most influential and acclaimed American glass artists, Dale Chihuly experiments with complex blown organic forms and brilliant colours, as seen in these vases: the three-piece Persian series sculpture (1986) and the lime green and red "Macchia" basket (1991), both one-off studio pieces that, like all his work, command high prices. £3,750–6,250/$6,000–10,000 (each)

Paperweights

Paperweights have always held a fascination for both glass enthusiasts and collectors in general, perhaps because of the way in which a flower or decorative pattern seems to be mysteriously magnified below a dome of clear glass. The classic design of paperweight features a *millefiori* (thousand flowers) pattern, made of densely packed sections of coloured glass rods, or canes, set into a base of clear glass and then sealed with a gather of molten glass. While this technique was known in 15thC Venice, the finest paperweights using this type of decoration were produced over a period of about 30 years in the mid-19thC by French factories, especially St Louis, Baccarat and Clichy. Different colours, shapes and arrangements of canes – often featuring silhouettes of birds, stars, roses, trefoils, insects and animals – are associated with particular firms. The 19thC vogue for naturalistic ornament is represented by the many weights depicting flowers, fruits, vegetables, butterflies and snakes. Some of the most expensive weights are those overlaid with white and coloured glass and cut with facets, showing the design inside. Paperweights, often in imitation of the French style, were produced in Britain, the United States and Bohemia in the mid-19thC in a range of styles, and are generally more affordable than the much rarer French examples. Paperweight techniques are also found on decorative and useful wares, including inkwells, scent bottles and vases, which are becoming increasingly collectable.

FRENCH

Paperweights produced by the French glassmaking factories of Baccarat, St Louis and Clichy during the 1840s are generally regarded as some of the finest ever made. They can be grouped into two main categories: *millefiori* weights and subject weights. *Millefiori* weights consist of a base made of clusters of multi-coloured glass "canes" encased in clear glass. Subject weights incorporate highly naturalistic flowers, fruit, animals, insects and birds, created by manipulating glass rods over an open flame or lamp. All French weights are highly collectable, and value is usually determined by rarity of colour or design.

◀ **SNAKE WEIGHT**
Baccarat snake and lizard weights are particularly rare today. This weight features a large pink snake with a dark-coloured eye lying coiled on a ground of close-packed white *latticinio* rods – often called a "muslin" ground.
£5,000–6,250/
$8,000–10,000

▶ **BUTTERFLIES WITH FLOWERS**
This weight includes a butterfly with the typical Baccarat dark-purple body and antennae, hovering over a large clematis flower with a cluster of green leaves. The marbled appearance of the butterfly's wings is also typical of the factory.
£1,500–1,750/
$2,400–2,800

▶ **CLICHY SWIRL**
This is among
the most distinctive
Clichy patterns:
it features white
staves alternating
with a single
colour. The central
motif consists of a
cluster of *millefiori*
rods in a star pattern.
£3,750–5,000/
$6,000–8,000

▶ **CLICHY INKWELL**
The French factories
also used paperweight-
making techniques to
create another range of
decorative wares. This
brass-mounted inkwell
is set with garlands
of white, purple, green
and pink *millefiori* canes
on a turquoise ground.
£3,750–5,000/
$6,000–8,000

◀ **BUNCH
OF GRAPES**
Brightly coloured fruit
weights are among the
most notable of those
made by the St Louis
factory. The most
common fruits are
grapes – shown in this
faceted weight – pears,

cherries and apples,
often with leaves. The
grapes in this weight
are shown on a clear
base, but in many
St Louis fruit weights
the fruits are laid in an
opaque-white *latticinio*
basket. £3,750–5,000/
$6,000–8,000

**OVERLAY
PAPERWEIGHTS**
*The term "overlay"
refers to a type of
weight coated with
a layer of white glass
overlaid with a layer
of blue, green or pink
glass and cut with up
to six facets revealing
the design within.
These were made
by all three French
factories in the mid-
19thC. Baccarat
glassmakers tended
to favour* **millefiori**
*patterns, while those
at St Louis preferred
bouquets of flowers with
leaves.* £7,500–9,375/
$12,000–15,000

St Louis overlays
commonly have six
facets with one on top,
while Baccarat and
Clichy examples
have five.

Apple
green is
an unusual
overlay
colour and
will enhance
the value of
the weight.

Bouquets of flowers,
buds and leaves are
characteristic of
St Louis.

The central clematis
flower reflects the 19thC
vogue for extremely
realistic depictions
of nature; other
favoured flowers
in paperweights
were pansies
and dahlias.

Bases are often star-cut
or strawberry diamond-cut

The coloured layer of
opaque glass is encased
in clear glass, known as
a double overlay.

OTHER

While the highest-quality weights were made by the three major French factories, a number of firms elsewhere in Europe and in the USA also produced weights from the 1850s to 1900. In England the Whitefriars Glassworks in London and George Bacchus & Son of Birmingham created *millefiori* paperweights, inkwells, door-knobs and scent bottles. For the Scottish factories Caithness and Moncrieff's Glass Works, the Spanish-born Paul Ysart (*b*.1904) produced designs featuring flowers, fish,

insects and butterflies. Paperweight production flourished in the USA from the early 1850s, especially after craftsmen from the leading French factories emigrated there. The leading exponents were the New England Glass Co. of East Cambridge, the Boston & Sandwich Glass Co. of Sandwich, the Mount Washington Glass Company of East Boston (all in Massachusetts) and Gillinder & Sons of Philadelphia. American and British weights are generally less expensive than the best French pieces.

◄ POINSETTIA DESIGN
Although better known for its press-moulded glass, the Boston & Sandwich Glass Company of Massachusetts made paperweights from *c*.1852 to 1888. The Boston & Sandwich glassmakers specialized in designs of flowers, especially poinsettias (shown in this weight), wheat-flowers and roses, as well as *millefiori* patterns incorporating canes with

silhouettes of wildlife, such as bees, rabbits and eagles. This colourful weight typically features a large central white-spotted crimson flower with a yellow-cane centre surrounded by a cluster of leaves and alternating smaller blue and crimson poinsettias around the edge. Boston & Sandwich weights can be distinguished by their relatively light weight and the varying quality of the clear glass and lampwork.
£500–625/$800–1,000

MAGNUMS & MINIATURES
Size can be a determining factor in the value of a paperweight. Most weights measure between 5 and 10cm (2–4in) in diameter; weights over 10cm/4in in diameter are known as magnums, and those less than 5cm/2in as miniatures. Both types, made by most of the major firms, are highly sought after today.

► NATURALISTIC APPLE
The New England Glass Company was the earliest producer (from 1850) of paperweights in the USA. Its fruit weights are among its best designs, but the firm is also known for flower and *millefiori* weights inspired by French examples. This New England example features a naturalistically moulded and coloured apple on a clear-glass base. £500–625/$800–1,000

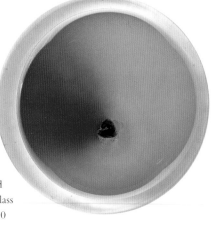

◀ APPLES AND CHERRIES
This New England Glass Company weight incorporates a group of fruits set among leaves on a white *latticinio* ground. Similar grounds were used for New England flower weights. The bright-green colour and clearly delineated veins of the leaves are typical of the firm's designs.
£250–375/$400–600

▶ BOHEMIAN WEIGHT
These 19thC and early 20thC paperweights are often engraved on the base; this weight has a typical amber-flashed ground engraved with a design of a horse. The design is made by cutting through the thin layer of coloured glass to expose the clear glass underneath. The top and sides are faceted.
£250–375/$400–600

◀ MUTED COLOURS
Bacchus of Birmingham produced weights from 1848 to *c*.1850. The firm's best *millefiori* designs have concentric patterns of canes set around a central white floret. Colours are typically rose pink, turquoise and blue, and are more muted than those used by the leading French makers. The star canes around the edge of this weight are typical of its designs.
£300–450/$475–725

▶ PAUL YSART
Apprenticed at the St Louis factory, Paul Ysart moved to Scotland in 1915. His weights often feature mottled grounds, as in the purple ground of this piece, and butterfly and dragonfly motifs. His designs are usually signed "PY" in one of the canes. This weight has a brightly coloured dragonfly and scattered *millefiori* canes.
£375–500/$600–800

Most glassware available to collectors today relates to eating and drinking, but other decorative and useful household items have been made in glass. These range from elegant scent bottles with sophisticated decoration to more ordinary items such as rolling-pins and door stops, and can be particularly appealing to the glass enthusiast who wishes to build up a more specialized collection of wares according to use or technique. Some of the most impressive items are those made of cameo glass, inspired by the 19thC revival of interest in ancient Roman glassworking techniques. The manufacture of cameo glass required an exceptional degree of skill on the part of the glass engraver and so was employed only for the most luxurious and expensive decorative vases, scent bottles and plaques. Similarly inspired by Classical cameos were tassies and sulphides – cast opaque-white glass or ceramic medallions, the latter often incorporated as decorative elements in useful wares such as decanters, jugs and drinking glasses. The well-appointed Victorian household would have contained a range of useful glass items, such as fly traps, letter openers, inkwells and bulb vases, many of which survive today. Some of the most intriguing small glassware was that produced by glassmakers in provincial factories from glass left over at the end of the working day – hence the name "end-of-day" glass. Items such as rolling-pins, bells, flasks, animal figures and pipes (with striped, combed, flecked or looped decoration) represent a very different kind of glassmaking from that of the well-known factories producing luxury tableware. Valued principally for their decorative appeal, these items are widely sought after.

DESKWARE

The writing desk of a Victorian gentleman or lady would have contained a variety of useful items, the most widely collected of which are paperweights. Inkwells were mostly made in silver with matching trays but examples are found in glass, often with brass or silver mounts. Pounce pots were used for storing a type of fine sand (pounce) for drying ink and were often made as part of a set with ink pots. Other items included letter openers, page turners and seals engraved with crests or monograms. Such pieces must be in good condition to retain their value.

▶ **INKWELL**
Glass inkwells were made from the mid-18thC with detachable silver or brass covers, and were often set on silver or silver-plated trays with pierced upright partitions for holding the pots in place. This piece (*c*.1890) has a typically wide, heavy base for stability. Some are decorated with cutting, usually around or under the base so that spilt ink did not catch in the decoration. £200–300/ $325–475

SCENT BOTTLES AND INKWELLS
In the 19thC scent bottles and inkwells were often made in identical styles, and it can be difficult to distinguish them. However, the glass stoppers on scent bottles are usually decorated while those on inkwells are plain.

▶ **PAIR OF INKWELLS**
Inkwells were often carried in a
travelling set or fitted into a case.
This Bohemian pair (c.1800) was
probably designed to fit into a
piece of furniture, hence the lack
of stoppers. The gilded decoration
is on the shoulders of the pots,
as this would have been the only
part visible. Inkwells were mostly
made in pairs but they are rarely
found as such today.
£200–300/$325–475

◀ **ENGRAVED PAGE TURNER**
Page turners were used to turn
the pages of expensive books to
prevent acid and dirt in fingerprints from damaging the paper
and bindings. This page turner

with "rock-crystal" engraving
was made c.1870 by the French
factory Baccarat. This luxurious
item is among the rarer and more
valuable types of glass deskware.
£700–900/$1,125–1,450

◀ *MILLEFIORI* **ITEMS**
Many glass factories making
paperweights also employed
the *millefiori* technique on other
decorative and useful wares
such as scent bottles, decanters,
inkwells and vases. This item
with a *millefiori* base, made by
Whitefriars c.1880, may have
been for matches to be struck
against the serrated edge of
the sphere. Such items are
uncommon, but less expensive
than paperweights.
£300–400/$475–650

▶ **COLOURED SEAL**
This colourful French glass seal
(c.1860) would have been used
to impress the writer's personal
crest or monogram into sealing
wax on an envelope, though
this piece is engraved simply
with a cross-hatched pattern.

The striated effect imitates
hardstones, which have
been used since Classical
times as engraved seals.
Such items are mainly
collected today for their
decorative value only.
£80–125/$125–200

DOMESTICWARE

Hygienic, easy to clean and impervious to strong flavours, glass, although vulnerable, is an ideal material for domesticware, and there is a huge range of household glass available to collectors. Until comparatively recently it was largely earlier 19thC pieces that attracted interest, but increasingly the 20thC offers unexpected treasures, either in the form of cutting-edge design such as the innovative domesticware by such designers as Wilhelm Wagenfeld, or in the field of the glassware of the 1950s and 1960s that now forms an integral part of reconstructing the 'look' of a particular decade. Functional household glass is usually unmarked unless, like PYREX®, it is patented as a brand name.

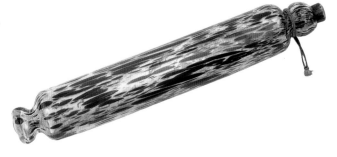

▶ GLASS ROLLING-PIN

These were given as love tokens, and many are decorated with girls' names and protestations of undying love. Made of bottle glass and decorated with "Nailsea"-style speckles and splashes, this one has a cork at one end, and originally may have been filled with salt. When empty it could be filled with cold water and used to work pastry. £80–100/$130–160

▶ NIGHT-LIGHT HOLDER

In the late 19thC vast numbers of glass night-light holders were made in a huge variety of styles. Samuel Clarke's patented pressed-glass "Fairy Light" bases were married with shades from various firms. This one would have been quite expensive as it has a Webb's "Queen's Burmese" shade, a type of shaded glass favoured by Queen Victoria. £100–150/$160–240

◀ HYACINTH-BULB VASE

Made c.1860, this vase was specifically designed to grow a hyacinth bulb, which sat in the cup-shaped top while its roots grew down into the water. Such vases were made in quantity during the 19thC and very early 20thC. They fell out of favour during both World Wars, but are now produced once more. The vases were made in a variety of styles: some in clear cut glass, others in coloured glass with elaborately shaped tops. Early original examples, normally with a narrow rim on top, are the most collectable, and coloured vases that conceal the roots are more popular than clear. £100–150/$160–240

◄ OIL LAMP

Although the refractive nature of glass made it an ideal medium for pre-electric lighting, few all-glass oil lamps exist as they were hard to make; the majority had glass reservoirs but metal or ceramic supporting columns. This example, made in Britain *c*.1870, is in excellent condition, and with its original cut-glass reservoir and base is one of the very attractive examples that are both collected in their own right and sometimes converted to electric use. £1,500–2,500/$2,400–4,000

PYREX®

One of the most practical domestic inventions of the 20thC was heat-resistant glass. It was first patented by the Corning Glassworks, New York, in 1915, and PYREX®, as it was called, became one of the largest markets in domestic glass, with British manufacturers such as Jobling buying manufacturing rights in 1921. Soon a range of heat resistant oven-to-tableware was being made in different forms, colours and patterns. PYREX® is readily found so must be in perfect condition; early pieces in shapes and patterns typical of a particular decade, such as the brightly coloured vegetables of the 1950s, are most collectable. Later pieces such as this are very inexpensive. £5–8/$8–12

▶ FLY TRAP

This traditional fly or wasp trap was probably made in England in the mid-19thC. The trough in the base was filled with sugar water or beer, the top was corked, and the insects flew in through a hole in the bottom and drowned in the liquid. This simple but effective design was made over a long period of time, well into the 20thC, and in many countries, including Spain and Portugal. Given that an unemptied trap would be most unappealing, it is surprising that coloured examples are rare. £70–90/$115–150

TASSIES & SULPHIDES

The fashion in the 18thC for Classically-inspired decorative cameos led the Scottish stonemason James Tassie (1735–99) to develop opaque-white glass portrait medallions in the mid-1760s. Usually representing politicians, royalty and other prominent contemporary figures, these medallions are known as tassies after their inventor and were made by modelling a portrait in wax, casting it in plaster, removing the wax and pouring a molten white glassy paste into the mould. Tassies continued to be made in London after James's death by his nephew William Tassie (1777–1860). The term "sulphide" refers to white ceramic medallions enclosed in clear glass. The first tentative experiments in producing sulphides were made in Bohemia in the mid-18thC, but in 1818 a method was patented in France by Pierre-Honoré Boudon de St-Amans (1774–1858). In England the leading producer of sulphides was Apsley Pellatt.

◀ THE GORGON'S HEAD

This white-glass medallion (date unknown) represents the Gorgon's Head and is based on Roman Imperial and ancient Greek sculpture – such Classical mythological subjects were popular decorative themes during the late 18thC and early 19thC, when the revival of interest in ancient Greece and Rome reached its peak. The background of this medallion is cast as one piece with the image, suggesting that it was made in the 19thC rather than the 18thC. £500–800/$800–1,275

▶ PORTRAITS

Most tassies represent well-known contemporary figures, such as the British statesman Edmund Burke, shown on the far right of these two examples of c.1800 by James Tassie (the other profile is of Jean Cross Clairmont). Early tassies feature the portrait medallion mounted on a sheet of glass of contrasting colour – in this case a bevelled, oval mount – to simulate true hardstone cameos. Later pieces were cast complete with a background. £825–1,000/$1,325–1,600

◀ ▶ GEORGE IV SULPHIDES

(Left) This sulphide plaque (*c.*1820) by Apsley Pellatt, featuring a portrait of King George IV after a painting by Sir Thomas Lawrence, is set in a gilt-metal frame and mounted on diamond-cut glass. Such finely executed plaques are among the most sought after sulphide pieces. £3,000–4,000/$4,800–6,400 (Right) Another portrait of George IV, this sulphide was made by Pellatt during the 1820s and is set in a glass frame, topped with a gilt-metal crown. £6,000–10,000/$9,600–16,000

◀ DECANTER STOPPER

As well as being made as decorative plaques, sulphides were also incorporated into a wide variety of useful glassware, such as decanters, jugs, goblets and tumblers. This square Regency decanter (*c.*1800) is set with a portrait medallion in the stopper, whereas on other examples the ceramic medallion is set in the side or on the base. The medallion often seems silvery rather than opaque white in appearance, owing to the very thin layer of trapped air formed during manufacture. £700–900/$1,125–1,440

▶ ORDER OF THE GARTER

While tassies generally depicted personalities, the subject matter of sulphides was much broader: it also included coats of arms, landscapes and, especially on French examples, religious scenes, such as images of the Madonna and Child. This sherry glass (1830) by Apsley Pellatt incorporates a sulphide representing the badge and motto of the Order of the Garter. £400–600/$640–950

SULPHIDES

Apsley Pellatt (1791–1863), owner of the Falcon Glassworks in London, patented the sulphide technique, which he called "crystallo-ceramie", in England in 1819, the year after St-Aman's patent in France. Although sulphides were also made in the USA, the leading producers were Bohemia, France and England.

SCENT BOTTLES

Scent bottles have been known since ancient Egyptian times, when small core-formed glass vessels were used for storing perfume. After the invention of mould-blowing in the 1stC AD the Romans produced a type of small glass bottle known as an *unguentarium* for containing aromatic oils. Produced in vast quantities – and often thrown away after use – such items are surprisingly quite common and reasonably priced today. The earliest modern European glass bottles were made in the 18thC and often embellished with lavish gilding, gold and silver mounts, enamelling, heavy cutting and cameo decoration, reflecting the high value of the scent. Before the mid-19thC scent was sold in simple commercial glass phials and decanted by the owner into his or her personal bottles. In the early 20thC notable glassmakers such as René Lalique designed a range of distinctive bottles for the major perfume and fashion houses; these are among the most collectable today.

◀ FITMENT FOR A TRAVELLING CASE
This Bohemian bottle (*c.*1800) would have been designed to lie flat in a lady's travelling case, and features gilt decoration of open roses – typical of late 18thC Bohemian glass, suggesting it could possibly have stored rosewater. However, the tall, slender shape of the bottle is often called an "Oxford Lavender", usually a relatively inexpensive type of bottle with a glass-peg stopper.
£150–250/$240–400

▶ GENTLEMAN'S SCENT BOTTLE
This English lead crystal bottle (*c.*1883) may have been made for a fashionable gentleman; it has relatively plain-cut trellis decoration and is large in size. The screw-on silver cap containing a glass stopper is a sign of good-quality craftsmanship.
£150–200/$240–325

▶ BOHEMIAN BLUE
Coloured glass was popular for scent bottles. As well as being decorative, it also helped to protect the scent from harmful ultra-violet light that could spoil the fragrance. The pale-blue opaline glass and heavy bulbous shape of this bottle *c.*1840 are Bohemian in style. Like many high-quality 19thC bottles it has a glass stopper inside the silver cap to keep the bottle airtight. £300–400/ $475–640

DOUBLE-ENDED BOTTLES
Portable double-ended scent bottles were popular in the late 19thC. They were often made of coloured glass with silver or silver-gilt mounts; the body was divided into two sections, one for perfume and one for smelling salts. These are the most affordable bottles available today.

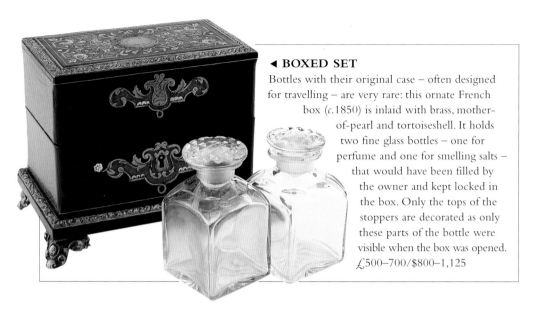

◀ BOXED SET

Bottles with their original case – often designed for travelling – are very rare: this ornate French box (*c*.1850) is inlaid with brass, mother-of-pearl and tortoiseshell. It holds two fine glass bottles – one for perfume and one for smelling salts – that would have been filled by the owner and kept locked in the box. Only the tops of the stoppers are decorated as only these parts of the bottle were visible when the box was opened. £500–700/$800–1,125

▶ ART DECO BOTTLE

The geometric rectangular body and cylindrical cap of this English bottle (1931) are particularly associated with the Art Deco style. The yellow enamel top of the cap is unusual – most examples have pink, green or blue enamel – and this will increase the value. The body is lightly engraved with flowers. Unlike 18th or early 19thC bottles, which usually fitted inside a travelling case, this would have formed part of a dressing-table set, with matching combs, brushes and mirror. £200–250/$325–400

◀ LUXURY BACCARAT BOTTLE

The technique of "rock-crystal" engraving, used only on the most expensive luxury glass items in the 19thC, such as this Baccarat bottle of *c*.1880, involved engraving the glass at an angle, then polishing the facets so that the finished product imitated carved natural rock crystal. The process was first employed by the English firm of Stevens & Williams in 1878, and used by Baccarat in France and Thomas G. Hawkes & Co. in the USA. The carving on the stopper matches that around the bottle, showing that the body and stopper were almost certainly made at the same time. £450–500/$725–800

CAMEO & INTAGLIO

Cameo – probably one of the most laborious and skilled decorative techniques in glass – describes two or more layers of glass of different colours, with the upper layer cut away to leave a relief design, often finely engraved, against a contrasting background. Imitating true hardstone cameos, the technique was first employed in ancient Rome to create such fine pieces as the Portland Vase (British Museum). This vase was brought to England from Italy in the late

18thC and, in the 19thC, inspired a fashion for cameo glass, of which the best-known English exponents were John Northwood (1836–1902) and George Woodall (1850–1925). The employment of Bohemian master engravers by English firms led, in the late 19thC, to the fashion for intaglio engraving – a technique originating in late 17thC Germany and Bohemia in which the glass surface is incised to varying depths to create complex three-dimensional effects.

◀ SCENT BOTTLE
Most cameo-glass wares are decorative pieces, such as vases and scent bottles, largely because the technique was too expensive to be used to decorate large suites of glass tableware. This scent bottle (1887) was made by Thomas Webb & Sons and is embellished with naturalistic flowers. Always check on pieces with a pattern around the neck that the carved design is complete – on some damaged pieces the rim has been ground down to remove chips and cracks. £800–1,000/$1,275–1,600

FRENCH CAMEO

While England was the leader in cameo glass, it was also made in France at the Baccarat and St Louis factories. These firms also became known for their *faux*, or acid-etched, cameo, in which acid was used to cut away the upper glass layer, though many pieces were finished by hand. At the turn of the century French glass artists, especially Emile Gallé (1846–1904), created innovatory cameo glass in the Art Nouveau style.

▲ INSPIRED BY ISLAMIC ART
Cameo glass normally features a pattern in white glass in relief against a coloured background, but this vase (*c.*1885) has an opaque ivory coloured body overlaid with carved ruby glass. The flattened form and the pattern of scrolls and flowers were inspired by Islamic art. The design is noted in one of Stevens & Williams' "Description Books" for April 1885. £925–1,250/$1,480–2,000

▶ QUALITY PIECE
The leaves and flowers embellishing this red-bodied vase are among the most usual types of cameo-glass decoration. The detail of the carving is of good quality, so that a piece like this will always command a high price. While some cameo glass is signed, unsigned pieces cannot be firmly attributed to one artist as many engravers moved from firm to firm or worked for several. £1,000–1,500/ $1,600–2,400

◀ FLOWERS AND PLANTS
This late 19thC English goblet, made of clear glass overlaid with green and engraved with a pattern of flowers and plants, is a fairly late example of "rock-crystal" intaglio engraved glass. However, the engraving on this piece is not of the highest quality. £100–125/$160–200

UNFINISHED PIECES
Incomplete cameo glass-items such as vases – usually lacking the fine definition found on finished examples – are quite widely available, though of lesser value. The work involved in carving cameo glass was so detailed that if the engraver made a small error the piece would often be abandoned.

◀ PRIZED PIECE
This vase (c.1880) showing Diana, goddess of the hunt, was executed by George Woodall, one of the leading English cameo-glass artists, who worked for Thomas Webb & Sons. Such pieces are highly prized by collectors because of the very fine engraved detail and the artist's signature incorporated into the design. While mythological subjects were felt particularly suitable for cameo glass, they were extremely complex and time-consuming, and so are usually found only on items made for exhibition. £5,000–10,000/$8,000–16,000

NAILSEA

Nailsea is a small town near Bristol, England, where a factory specializing in crown (window) glass and bottle glass was founded in the late 18thC. However, the factory became better known for domestic pieces such as jugs and decanters, flecked or striped in white or coloured glass, which supposedly were made there. "Nailsea" is now the general term for small decorative items in this style, made by glassmakers in their spare time from glass left over at the end of day. These were produced at glassworks in the Midlands and other provincial centres, and include items such as walking-sticks, bells, rolling-pins and witch balls (large silvered-glass spheres). While Nailsea glass is less sophisticated than contemporary cut and coloured glass, it is becoming increasingly collectable. The maker and/or factory can rarely be identified as Nailsea is not marked.

◀ LETTER OPENER
This letter opener in the form of a dagger, with a coloured-glass handle, was made by the factory of Val St Lambert in Belgium, established in 1825. The factory also made high-quality art glass and domestic wares.
£100–150/$160–240

▶ WIG STAND
Obelisk-shaped glass objects like this are often called wig stands – although it is unlikely that they were actually used for holding wigs. Two shapes are known – the spike version shown here and the ball top. The latter is more widely reproduced.
£100–150/$160–240

▲ DOG DOORSTOP
This white-glass model of a dog would have been used as a doorstop, originally made as one of a pair – matching pairs are worth more than twice a single example today. Most dog doorstops were made in green-tinted glass – cast in the same mould used to make more expensive cast-iron pieces – and this opaque-white example is thus quite rare.
£50–100/$80–160

NAILSEA BELLS
Bells are among the most popular items of Nailsea glass with collectors. The majority have coloured bodies – most commonly red ones – joined with plaster of Paris to clear-glass handles. Typical decoration includes knops on the handles and wrythen moulding or ribbing on the bodies.

◀ DOORSTOP
Among the most common types of useful ware made from left-over green crown glass are dumps, or doorstops, featuring internal bubble or tear, or plaster, decoration. Some commemorative pieces can be found, such as those celebrating Queen Victoria's jubilees. Bubbled examples have been widely copied, and it can be difficult to distinguish the originals from reproductions. As doorstops were subjected to heavy wear and tear, they are frequently damaged, with internal "bruises". £100–150/$160–240

◀ ORNAMENTEL DECANTER
Nailsea flasks and decanters, like this elegant stoppered decanter, generally feature looped white trailed or combed decoration, although pink and blue are also known. These were not generally intended to be used for serving wine and spirits, but were for ornament only. The long neck and high stopper are characteristic of 19thC decanter styles. £100–150/$160–240

▲ MODEL SHIP
Intricate and detailed small glass models of ships, which were often made by itinerant glassworkers to be sold at country fairs, are a *tour de force* of the art of lampwork. This process involves manipulating thin glass rods over an open flame. Models such as this one, above, with its turned wooden base and protective glass dome, are preferable, as without domes they can harbour dirt and are easily broken. Damaged pieces are virtually impossible to repair. £50–75/$80–125

PART 5

INFORMATION

ABOVE VALUABLE SOURCES OF INFORMATION ON
COLLECTING ANTIQUES.

LEFT A COLOURFUL DISPLAY OF CRANBERRY,
VASELINE AND IRIDESCENT VICTORIAN GLASS.

DESIGNERS & MANUFACTURERS

Baccarat

Muerthe, France. Most important contemporary maker of crystal. Founded 1764. Wide variety of products. Trademark registered 1860, still in use. Label or acid-etched:

George Bacchus & Son

Birmingham, England. Established c.1840. Influenced by Bohemian glass. Decorated opal ware, transfer-printed with black, sepia and polychrome. Signature on vase, c.1850:

Dominik Bieman

(1800–1857), Frazenbad, Bohemia. Worked in Vienna and Prague. Engraved scenes and portraits. Many spellings of name:

DOMINIK BIEMANN

Daum et Cie

Important glassworks in France. Established 1875. During each period, Daum produced a wide range of styles. In 1969 began to make a series of limited edition plates.

1895–1920:

George Davidson & Co.

Gateshead, England. Established 1867. Quality pressed, slag and other domestic wares. Signature moulded in ware:

Friedrich Egermann

(1777–1864) Born at Blottendorf, Bohemia. Established a workshop at Haida where he experimented with a variety of techniques. He patented "Lithyalin", a marbled, opaque glass, in 1828. Signatures on Lithyalin are rare and often obliterated. Egermann also discovered new methods of staining glass red and yellow. Signature on enamelled beaker:

F. E.

Cristallerie d'Emile Gallé

Nancy, France. Emile Gallé (1845–1904), was a leader of the Art Nouveau movement. Established his own glass house for art glass in 1867. Used marquetry, cameo, engraving, and other techniques for vases, lamps and tableware. Clear enamelled items showing Islamic and Venetian influences. Best known for carved and etched glass. Most wares high quality, individually decorated. Also produced a commercial line of acid-etched cameo for the popular market. Signature on cameo with many other

variations (below left): A star beside name (below right) denotes work produced after Gallé's death to represent the loss of one of France's shining stars, used from September 1904 until 1914:

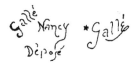

Mrs Graydon-Stannus

London, active 1923–32. Makers of decorative wares using opal glass, clear glass with applied decoration, Cluthra and flashed glass. Forgeries are reported.

Henry Greener & Co.

Established 1858, Sunderland, England. Late 19thC. Lacy, pressed (c.1870–80), slag, commemoratives, etc. Mark used from 1884. Signature moulded in pressed ware: mark left used 1875–85; mark right used c.1885–1900. Continental copies are unmarked.

Thomas G. Hawkes & Co.

Corning, New York. Registered trade name. Has been reported to be used as an acid stamp in block letters on wares other than Hawkes:

GRAVIC

Lalique

René Lalique (1860–1945), French glassmaker and jewellery designer, famous for his scent bottles. The Lalique glassworks also produced glass screens, lamps, car mascots, fountains and lights. Usually worked with frosted-white opalescent glass and rarely used colour. Used naturalistic motifs for decoration, including fish, animals, flowers, leaves and fruit. After his death his son, Marc, continued the business as "Cristal Lalique", and modern pieces are marked "Lalique, France".

Engraved signature:

Impressed mark:

[ALIQUE]

J. & L. Lobmeyr

Signature engraved or enamelled. Used after 1860:

⊞

Moncrieff's Glass Works

Perthshire, Scotland. John Moncrieff in c.1922 began to make decorative wares. "Monart" glass was developed in 1924 by Salvador Ysart (1887–1956). Made only by him and his son Paul. The glass is clear, heavy, streaked with black, scarlet and other Art Deco colours. Maker of paperweights. Contemporary line of art glass called "Monax":

Trademark on paper label. One reference reports the original to be green, another reports the label as gold with black:

Mount Washington Glass Co.
South Boston, Massachusetts. Established 1837, resumed original name 1871. Acquired by Pairpoint, *c.*1894. Mould-blown and pressed art glass: "Burmese", "Royal Flemish", cut glass etc. Trademark: original is a paper label. Forgeries made of same form are acid-etched. "Royal Flemish" ware gives an appearance of stained-glass sections separated by raised gilt lines:

W. H., B. & J. Richardson
Wordsley, England, *c.*1836–50 when it became Henry G. Richardson & Sons (see below). Signature: enamel decoration and signature. Early decorations were black, later polychrome. One piece of each set was signed:

RICHARDSON'S VITRIFIED

RICHARDSON'S VIRTIFIED ENAMEL COLOURS

Compagnie des Cristalleries de St Louis
Münzthal, Lorraine. Wide range of fine crystal items made up to present day. Trademark:

Etched on cameo vase:

ST LOUIS, NANCY

Sowerby & Neville (1855–72); Sowerby & Co. (1872–81); Sowerby Ellison Glassworks (1881–).
Gateshead, England. Inexpensive pressed, slag, spangled, etc. Marked from 1876 onwards. Signature moulded in ware, usually under base, sometimes in interior. May also have registry mark:

Steuben Glass Works
Established 1903 by Frederick Carder in Corning, New York. Taken over by Corning Glass Works in 1918. Mark 1903–32 was acid-stamped fleur-de-lys with "Steuben" on a scroll. Mark after 1932:

Stevens & Williams
England, 19thC makers of art glass. Signature in cameo on acid cut-back vase, at bottom:

Tiffany Furnaces
Corona, N.Y. Trademark registered 1902, used only as a label. Never etched on glass wares:

Patented 1912. Trade name not used as a

permanent mark on *Fabrique* glass panels in lamp shades.

Tiffany Glass and Decorating Co.
New York, N.Y. 1892–1902. Established by Louis Comfort Tiffany. Leaded windows, art-glass lamps and vases. Trademark issued 13 November 1894, used as a paper label embossed in green and gold, or printed in black and white. May read *Favrile* or *Fabrile*. Printed labels may have glass type between *Favrile* and Glass – for example, "Sunset". This monogram was not used as an etched signature:

Tiffany Glass Co.
1886–92, rare signature may be acid stamped in pontil. Beware of forgeries:

Tiffany Studios
Formerly the Tiffany Glass and Decorating Co. (above). New York, N.Y. Trademark registered *c.*1904, but in use after 1902. Undertook interior design commissions and expanded to make a wide range of items in many different materials, including glass, using innovative techniques. Studios closed after Tiffany's death in 1933. Paper label, not acid stamp:

Tiffany & Co.
New York, N.Y. Retail jewellers, established 1834 by Tiffany's father Charles Lewis Tiffany. Mark used on wares retailed in New York store:

Waterford Crystal Ltd
Waterford, Ireland. Opened 1951. Maker of quality stemware, lamps. Trademark:

Thomas Webb & Sons
John Shepherd & Thos. Webb at White House Glass Works 1833–40. Thos. Webb's glassworks "The Flats", 1840–55; Thos. Webb, Dennis Glass Works, 1835–59; Thos. Webb & Sons, Dennis Glass Works, 1859 onwards. Signature engraved on cameo work:

THOS. WEBB & SON

Acid-etched on Burmese Ware:

Other signatures on cameo pieces:

THOMAS WEBB & SONS/

THOS. WEBB & SONS

Thomas and George Woodall
England, established by brothers Thomas (1849–1926) and George (1850–1925). Cameo carvers at Thomas Webb & Sons. Signature 1880–1900:

J & G Woodall

WHERE TO BUY & SEE

WHERE TO BUY

Glass can be purchased through many sources, including auction houses, antiques dealers, markets, fairs and car-boot sales. Below is just a selection of useful names and addresses to start you off.

MAJOR AUCTION HOUSES

Bonhams Chelsea
65–9 Lots Road
London SW10
www.bonhams.com

The Frank Boos Gallery
420 Enterprise Court
Bloomfield Hills,
MI USA

Christie's London
8 King Street, St James's
London SW1
www.christies.com

Christie's New York
Rockefeller Center
20 Rockefeller Plaza
New York City, NY USA

Green Valley Auctions
2259 Green Valley Lane
Mt Crawford, VA USA

Phillips
101 New Bond Street
London W1Y 2AA
www.phillips-auctions.com

Skinner
357 Main Street
Bolton, MA USA

Sotheby's
34-35 New Bond Street
London W1A
www.sothebys.com

Sotheby's New York
1334 York Avenue
New York City, NY USA

SPECIALIST DEALERS

Contact a major trade association or see listings in antiques fairs catalogues.

Artemis
36 Kensington Church Street, London W8

Nigel Benson
58-60 Kensington Church Street, London W8

The Ginnell Gallery Antiques Centre
18-22 Lloyd Street
Manchester M2

Grimes House Antiques
High Street,
Moreton-in-Marsh,
Glos GL56

Jeanette Hayhurst
32a Kensington
Church Street,
London W8

Lillian Nassau
220 East 57th Street
New York City, NY
USA

Mark West
39b High Street
Wimbledon
London SW19

Sweetbriar Gallery (International Paperweight Dealers)
Sweetbriar House,
Robin Hood Lane
Helsby, Frodsham
Cheshire WA6

ANTIQUES FAIRS

Alexandra Palace Antiques and Collectors' Fair
Alexandra Palace
London N22
(September)

Antiques for Everyone
National Exhibition Centre
Birmingham B40 (April)

BADA Fair
Duke of York's
Headquarters,
Chelsea
London SW3 (March)

Baltimore Museum Antiques Show
Baltimore Museum of Art
10 Art Museum Drive
Baltimore, MD USA

Chelsea Antiques Fair
Chelsea Old Town Hall
King's Road,
London SW3
(March/September)

Connecticut Spring Antiques Show
State Armory
Hartford, CT USA

Fall Show at the Armory
Seventh Regiment
Armory
67th Street & Park Avenue
New York City, NY
USA

The Grosvenor House Antiques Fair
Grosvenor House Hotel,
Park Lane
London W1A (June)

Harrogate Antiques and Fine Art Fair
Harrogate International
Centre
Harrogate
Yorkshire HG1 (April)

LAPADA Antiques Fair
The Royal
College of Art,
Kensington Gore
London SW7 (January)

International Fine Art and Antique Dealers Show
Seventh Regiment Armory
67th Street & Park Avenue
New York City, NY USA

The Newark International Antiques and Collectors' Fair
The Newark &
Nottinghamshire
Showground, Newark
NG24 (April/June/August)

New York Winter Antiques Show
Seventh Regiment Armory
67th Street & Park Avenue
New York City, NY USA

Olympia Fine Art & Antiques Fair
Hammersmith Road
London W14
(February/June)

Original National Glass Collectors' Fair
National Motorcycle
Museum, Birmingham
B92 (November)

Philadelphia Antiques Show
103rd Engineers Armory
33rd & Market Streets
Philadelphia PA USA

Riverside Antiques Show
New Hampshire State
Armory, Canal Street
Manchester, NH USA

San Francisco Fall Antiques Show
Fort Mason Center
San Francisco, CA USA

Thames Valley Antiques Dealers Association Fair
The Blue Coat School
Sonning-on-Thames
Berkshire (April)

**Washington
Antiques Show**
Omni Shorham Hotel
2500 Calvert Street
Washington DC USA

**West London
Antiques Fair**
Kensington Town Hall
Hornton Street
London W8
(January/August)

**Westminster
Antiques Fair**
Royal Horticultural
Hall, Vincent Square
London SW1 (January)

**ANTIQUES MARKETS
& CENTRES**

Alfies Antiques Market
13-25 Church Street
Marylebone
London NW8 8DT

Antiquarius
King's Road, Chelsea
London SW3

Assembly Antique Centre
5-8 Saville Row, Bath
Somerset BA1

Bath Antiques Market
Guinea Lane, Landsdown
Road, Bath Somerset BA1

Bermondsey Market
Bermondsey Street
London SE1 (Friday)

**Brimfield Antiques
Market**
Brimfield, MA USA

Bristol Antiques Market
The Exchange
Corn Street, Bristol BS1

Camden Passage
Upper Street
Islington, London N1
(Tuesday–Saturday)

Chenil Galleries
181 King's Road
Chelsea, London SW3

Newark Antiques Centre
Lombard Street
Newark NG24

**Portobello Road
Market**
Portobello Road
London W11 (Saturday)

WHERE TO SEE
Visiting major collections
in museums and houses
open to the public is
an invaluable way to
learn more about glass.
Listed below are places
with important glass
collections to visit.

British Museum
Great Russell Street
London WC1

**Broadfield House
Glass Museum**
Kingswinford
West Midlands DY6

Burrell Collection
Pollokshaws Road
Glasgow G43

Chrysler Museum
Norfolk, VA USA

**Corning Museum
of Glass**
Corning, NY USA

Fitzwilliam Museum
Trumpington Street
Cambridge CB2

Geffrye Museum
Kingsland Road
London E2

**Harvey's Wine
Museum**
12 Denmark Street
Bristol BS1

Laing Art Gallery
New Bridge Street
Newcastle upon Tyne
NE1 8AG

**The Metropolitan
Museum of Art**
1000 Fifth Avenue
New York City, NY USA

Museum of London
London Wall
London EC2Y

**Norwich Castle
Museum**
Norwich City, Norfolk

Rijks Museum
Stadhouderskade 42
Amsterdam
The Netherlands

Royal Ontario Museum
100 Queen's Park
Toronto, Ontario Canada

Sandwich Glass Museum
Sandwich MA USA

**Toledo Museum
of Glass**
Toledo, OH USA

Ulster Museum
Botanic Gardens
Belfast BT9
Northern Ireland

**Victoria and
Albert Museum**
Cromwell Road
London SW7

World of Glass
Chalon Way East
St Helens
Lancs WA10

SOCIETIES & CLUBS

Antique Collectors' Club
5 Church Street,
Woodbridge
Suffolk IP12 1DS

**Cambridge
Paperweight Circle**
56 Manor Drive North,
New Malden
Surrey KT3 5NY

**The Carnival Glass
Society (UK)**
P.O. Box 14, Hayes
Middlesex UB3 5NU

**Paperweight
Collectors
Association, Inc.**
P.O. Box 1263,
Beltsville, MD USA

**UK Perfume Bottles
Collectors Club**
Lynda Brine
Assembly Antique Centre
5-8 Saville Row, Bath
Somerset BA1 2QP

ASSOCIATIONS
Trade associations offer
helpful information on
annual antiques fairs,
specialist dealers, valuations
and insurance.

**Art and Antique
Dealers' League of
America (AADLA)**
1040 Madison Avenue
New York City, NY USA

**London and
Provinical Antique
Dealers' Association
(LAPADA)**
535 King's Road
London SW10

**British Antique
Dealers' Association
(BADA)**
20 Rutland Gate
London SW7

**National Antique and
Art Dealers Association
of America (NAADAA)**
220 East 57th Street
New York City, NY USA

WHAT TO READ

GENERAL BOOKS

Battie, David & Cottle, Simon,
Sotheby's Concise Encyclopedia, 1991
Bray, Charles, *Dictionary of Glass:
Materials & Techniques*, 1995
British Museum, *Masterpieces
of Glass*, 1968
Davis, Derek C., *Glass for
Collectors*, 1971
Dodsworth, Roger, *Glass
and Glassmakers*, 1982
Drahotova, Olga, *European Glass*, 1983
Hajdamach, Charles, *British Glass
1800–1914*, 1991
Haynes, E. Barrington, *Glass
Through the Ages*, 1970
Janneau, Guillaume,
Modern Glass, 1931
Klein, Dan & Lloyd, Ward,
The History of Glass, 1984
Liefkes, Reino, ed., *Glass*, 1997
Miller, Judith (General Editor),
Miller's Antiques Encyclopedia, 1998
Miller, Muriel M., *Glass*, 1990
Morris, Barbara, *Victorian Table Glass
and Ornaments*, 1978
Newman, Harold, *An Illustrated
Dictionary of Glass*, 1977
Pfaender, Heinz G., *Schott Guide
to Glass*, 1996
Stennett-Willson, Ronald,
Modern Glass, 1975
Tait, Hugh, ed., *Five Thousand
Years of Glass*, 1995
West, Mark, *Miller's Antiques
Checklist: Glass*, 1994
Wilson, Kenneth M., *American
Glass 1760–1930*, 1994

SPECIALIST BOOKS

Arwas, Victor, *Art Nouveau to Art
Deco – The Art of Glass*, 1996
Bacri, C., *Daum: Masters of French
Decorative Glass*, 1993
Beard, Geoffrey, *International
Modern Glass*, 1976
Beck, Doreen, *The Book of Bottle
Collecting*, 1973
Bickerton, L.M., *18th Century
English Drinking Glasses:
An Illustrated Guide*, 1986
Bickerton, L.M., *English Drinking
Glasses 1675–1825*, 1987

Boggess, Bill & Louise, *Identifying
American Brilliant Cut Glass*, 1991
Broizova, J., *Bohemian Crystal*, 1984
Butler, Robin & Walkling, Gillian,
Book of Wine Antiques, 1996
Charleston, Robert J., *English
Glass and the Glass used in
England c. 400–1940*, 1984
Cooke, Frederick, *Glass – Twentieth
Century Design*, 1986
Cummings, K, *Techniques of
Kiln-Formed Glass*, 1997
Curtis, J-L., *Baccarat*, 1992
Davis, Derek C., *English Bottles
& Decanters 1650–1900*, 1972
Dawes, N.M., *Lalique Glass*, 1986
Dodsworth, Roger, ed., *British Glass
Between the Wars*, 1987
Duncan, Alastair & Bartha, G.,
Glass by Gallé, 1984
Dunlop, Paul, *The Jokelson Collection
of Antique Cameo Incrustations*, 1991
Edwards, Bill, *Standard Encyclopedia
of Opalescent Glass*, 1995
Elville, E., *English Table Glass*, 1951
Frothingham, Alice Wilson,
Spanish Glass, 1964
Gardner, Paul V., *The Glass of
Frederick Carder*, 1971
Grover, Ray & Lee,
Art Nouveau Glass, 1967
Hollingworth, Jane,
Collecting Decanters, 1980
Husfloen, Kyle, *Collector's Guide to
American Pressed Glass 1825–1915*,
1992
Jackson, Lesley, *20th Century
Factory Glass*, 2000
Jackson, Lesley, *Whitefriars Glass*, 1997
Lattimore, Colin R., *English 19th
Century Press-Moulded Glass*, 1979
Leibe, Frankie, *Miller's Glass of the
'20s & '30s: A Collector's Guide*, 1999
Mackay, J. *Glass Paperweights*, 1973
Melvin, Jean S., *American Glass
Paperweights and their Makers*, 1970
Metcalfe, Anne, *Miller's Paperweights
of the 19th & 20th Centuries:
A Collector's Guide*, 2000
Norman, Barbara,
Glass Engraving, 1987
Notley, Raymond, *Miller's Popular
Glass of the 19th & 20th Centuries:
A Collector's Guide*, 2000
Olivié, Jean-Luc & Petrova, Sylvia,

Bohemian Glass, 1990
O'Looney, E. *Victorian Glass*, 1972
Opie, Jennifer, *Scandinavia:
Ceramics and Glass in the
Twentieth Century*, 1989
Palmer, Arlene, *Glass in Early
America: Selections from the
Henry Francis Du Pont Winterthur
Museum*, 1994
Polak, Ada, *Modern Glass*, 1962
Porter, Norman & Jackson,
Douglas, *Tiffany Glassware*, 1988
Revi, Albert Christian, *American
Cut & Engraved Glass*, 1965
Sheppard & Smith, John P.,
Engraved Glass, 1991
Sheppard & Smith, John P., *From
the Restoration to the Regency*, 1990
Slack, Raymond, *English Pressed
Glass 1830–1900*, 1987
Smith, John P., *Osler's Crystal
for Royalty and Rajahs*, 1991
Smith, John P., *The Art of
Enlightenment*, 1994
Spiegl, Walter, *Glas des
Historismus*, 1980
Spillman, Jane Shadel, *American
& European Pressed Glass in the
Corning Museum of Glass*, 1981
Spillman, Jane Shadel,
*The American Cut-Glass Industry
and T.G. Hawkes*, 1996
Spillman, Jane Shadel & Frantz,
Susanne K., *Masterpieces of American
Glass: The Corning Museum of Glass,
the Toledo Museum of Art, Lillian
Nassau Ltd.*, 1990
Swan, Martha Louise, *American Cut
and Engraved Glass: The Brilliant
Period in Historical Perspective*, 1994
Tait, Hugh, *Golden Age of Venetian
Glass*, 1979
Wakefield, Hugh, *Nineteenth
Century Glass*, 1961
Warren, Phelps, *Irish Glass*, 1970
Warthorst, Karl-Wilhelm,
Theresienthal, 2000
Webb Lee, Ruth, *Early American
Pressed Glass*, 1966
Webb Lee, Ruth, *Sandwich Glass:
The History of the Sandwich Glass
Co.*, 1966
Welker, John, *Pressed Glass in
America: Encyclopedia of the First
Hundred Years, 1825–1925*, 1985

GLOSSARY

Acid-etching Technique involving treatment of glass with acid, giving a matt or frosted finish.

Acid polishing Process creating a shiny finish by dipping the glass into a mixture of hydrofluoric and sulphuric acids.

Annealing Slow cooling of hot glass that reduces internal stresses that may cause cracking once glass is cold.

Aventurine From the Italian for "chance"; decoration of flecked metallic particles.

Baluster 18thC drinking glass with a stem based on the baluster, a form derived from Renaissance architecture.

Balustroid A taller, lighter form of baluster.

Biedermeier A bourgeois style that influenced all the decorative arts in Germany *c.*1825–40; the glass is characterized by the quality and range of its colours.

Blowing Technique of producing glass vessels by blowing a molten mass of glass, or gather, through a blowpipe or blowing iron, either freehand or into a mould.

Bristol blue Generic description for rich blue glass, coloured using cobalt oxide.

Burmese glass An opaque heat-sensitive glass.

Cameo glass Decorative carved, cased or flashed glass with two or more different-coloured layers, so the carved design stands out in relief.

Core-forming Technique of producing a glass vessel by shaping trails of molten glass over a core usually made from mud or clay, and fusing them together in a furnace; the core is carved or acid-etched out when cool.

Canes Rods of glass drawn out by the glass blower to a required thickness for use as decoration.

Carnival glass Pressed or blow-moulded glass that is sprayed with metallic salts when hot to produce a shimmering iridescent effect.

Cased glass Pieces made of two or more layers of coloured decoration sandwiched between two layers of clear glass.

Cristallo Type of soda glass developed in 15thC Venice, made with soda from the ashes of the barilla plant.

Crizzling A network of tiny cracks fogging the surface of a piece, caused by an imbalance in the glass batch.

Custard glass A creamy-coloured uranium glass made opaque with white oxides.

Cutting Decoration, either polished or matt, created by offering the piece to a stone wheel at varying angles.

Daumenglas A traditional German cylindrical or barrel-shaped beaker.

Depression Glass American mechanically moulded suites of table glass with shallow patterns, dating from the 1930s and 1940s.

Diamond-point engraving Line-drawing on a glass surface using a diamond or metal point; designs comprising a series of dots rather than lines using this type of tool are called stipple engraving.

Eiserot see Schwarzlot.

Enamelling Decorative technique using coloured glass ground to a powder and mixed with an oily substance that is painted onto the glass and reheated to fuse the design to the surface.

Engraving Lightly abraded, matt surface decoration created with a fine copper wheel.

Faceting Technique used to decorate curved glass surfaces by grinding to make flat, geometric sections.

Façon de Venise French, meaning "in the Venetian style", used to describe high-quality, Venetian-influenced glassware made in Europe during the 16thC & 17thC.

Faience Substance made from finely-ground quartz (a form of silica) covered with glass-like vitreous glaze.

Filigrana Italian, meaning "thread-grained"(called filigree in English), used to describe many variations of a decorative style that incorporates threads of (usually opaque-white) glass inside a clear-glass body in a variety of lattice patterns.

Flashed Method of colouring glass that involves applying a thin layer of coloured glass to a vessel, either

by painting it or dipping it into a pot of colorant; flashed glass can be carved to produce a less expensive version of overlay glass.

Flint glass Alternative name for clear glass.

Flux An alkaline substance added to the glass batch to aid fusion of ingredients.

Gather The mass of molten glass attached to the end of a blowpipe or pontil rod before a vessel is formed.

Gilding A technique of glass decoration that involves painting the glass surface with gold leaf, gold dust or gold paint and then firing to fix the design. Gilt decoration that is not fired is known as "cold gilding" and is less hard-wearing.

Historismus European revival, *c.*1870, of the production of old Venetian and traditional German glass forms from the 15th and 16thC.

Humpen Tall cylindrical German beer glass made from the mid-16thC to the 18thC.

"In front of the kiln" Phrase used to describe applied decoration added by hand to a hot glass object.

Iridescence A thin layer of metallic salts applied to glass to produce lustres.

Jacobite glass 18thC glassware engraved in support of the Jacobite pretenders to the English throne.

Kick Indentation in the base of a glass vessel.

Knops Swellings, which can be solid or hollow, that occur in a variety of forms on glass stems.

Kuttrolf Antique German bottle for spirits such as schnapps, with a large surface area for cooling.

Lacy glass Type of US pressed glass with a stipple-engraved background that gives a lacy effect.

Lampwork Glass that is blown or manipulated from clear or coloured glass rods over a blow lamp or torch.

Lattimo From the Italian *latte*, meaning "milk"; an opaque-white glass made by adding bone ash or tin oxide to the glass batch. Also known as Milk glass.

Latticinio or *Latticino* Other Italian terms used to describe *filigrana*.

Lead crystal Glass made using a large proportion of lead oxide that was not vulnerable to crizzling, first made by George Ravenscroft in the late 17thC.

"Lost-wax" casting Technique in which a wax model is cased in plaster and the wax then steamed out ("lost") to make a mould for *pâte-de-cristal* and *pâte-de-verre*; also known as *cire perdue*.

Lustres Metal oxides suspended in oil used for painting onto hot glass.

Malachite A marble-effect opaque pressed glass.

Marigold Term describing a golden iridescence added onto clear glass.

Marvering An ancient technique where hot threads of softened glass are rolled over a flat table (a marver) to smooth and fuse the glass, and to fix trailed decoration.

Metal Term used to describe hot or cold glass.

Millefiori Italian word, meaning "a thousand flowers"; used to describe mosaic patterns created by horizontal sections of rods of coloured glass often found in paperweights.

Mitre-cutting Deep, V-shaped cuts.

Mould, metal Expensive durable iron moulds, finely cut and chased.

Mould, wood Less durable (but cheaper) hinged moulds for mould-blown hollow glass.

Mould-blowing *see* blowing.

Nailsea glass Items of novelty glass, such as walking-sticks, flasks and bells, made near Bristol in the 18thC and 19thC.

Ormolu Gilded bronze decoration.

Opalescent glass A type of glass that appears to have fiery internal highlights.

Optic Decoration within, or on the surface of, the glass that reflects the lighting patterns.

Overlay glass Also known as cased glass: a technique in which a glass body is covered by one or more differently coloured outer layers that may be carved in a relief design.

Paraison Bubble of molten glass on the end of a pontil rod or blowpipe that has been partially inflated.

Pâte-de-cristal French term meaning "crystal paste": translucent glassware made from very finely powdered glass made into a paste and shaped using the "lost-wax" method.

Pâte-de-verre French term meaning "glass paste": opaque pieces made from a paste of crushed glass and using the "lost-wax" method.

Peach opal(escent) A term describing clear opalescent glass to which golden iridescence is added.

Pontil mark Rough patch or mark at the base of a vessel, left when the pontil rod is detached.

Pontil rod Rod that is attached to the base of a vessel to hold it steady while it is finished, after it is blown.

Potash glass Strong type of glass made from potash, lime and silica. Also called *verre de fougère* or *Waldglas* (see below).

Press-moulded or pressed glass Technique that involves pouring molten glass into a metal mould and pressing it to the sides using a metal plunger; a mechanized version of this process was first developed in the United States in c.1820.

Prunts Blobs of glass applied to a glass surface as a decorative technique.

Queensware Opaque, warm-cream vitro-porcelain *(see below)* glass that imitated later 18thC creamware. Name borrowed from Wedgwood by Sowerby glassmakers.

Rock-crystal engraving Form of engraving where a clear-glass surface is highly polished to imitate the mineral rock crystal

Roemer Traditional German drinking vessel with an ovoid bowl and a cylindrical stem with applied prunts and a spreading foot.

Rubinglas German, "ruby glass": richly-coloured red glass created by adding copper or gold oxide to the glass mix.

Rummer 19thC English low drinking goblet, traditionally used for drinking rum and water.

Schwarzlot 17thC German technique of freehand painting on glass using translucent black enamel; an iron-red enamel called *eiserot* was also used.

Silica Fine sand, the basic raw material for glass. Melts at very high temperature and therefore requires fluxes (like soda) to reduce melting temperature to a practical level.

Soda glass Light, malleable glass with a faint brown or greenish tinge. Made using sodium carbonate as a flux, it has no lead content and does not ring when struck; *see cristallo*.

Staining A method of colouring glass by painting the surface with metal oxide, and reheating to fix the colour.

Stipple engraving *see* diamond-point engraving.

Star-cutting Multiple cuts meeting at a central point to create a star pattern.

Studio glass One-off pieces designed and produced by usually independent artist-craftsmen.

Tazza Italian for "cup": a decorative cup or dish with a foot, used to serve food but also for decoration.

Tear Drop-shaped air bubble enclosed in a glass, usually the stem.

Trailing Decorative technique where strands of glass are drawn out from a gather and trailed over a glass surface.

Transfer print A design printed on paper from an engraved copper plate and applied to the surface of the glass.

Vaseline glass Acidically coloured green or yellow glass.

Verre de soie French for "satin glass": a type of glass with a satin finish

Vetro a fili Italian "thread glass"; a type of *filigrana*. Other types include *vetri a reticello* (glass with a small network), *vetri a retortoli* (glass with a twist) and *vetri di trino* (lace glass).

Vitro-porcelain Glass which appears at first glance to be ceramic.

Waldglas German "forest glass"; green-coloured glass made with a potash (potassium carbonate) flux that is derived from the ashes of burned wood or ferns. In France it is known as *verre de fougère*.

INDEX

ACKNOWLEDGMENTS

The publishers would like to thank the following dealers, collectors and auction houses for supplying pictures for use in this book or for allowing their pieces to be photographed. The author would like to thank Mark West for his expertise, Frankie Leibe and Jill Bace for their editorial contributions and Emily Anderson at Mitchell Beazley for her patience, editorial skills and good humour throughout this project.

Front jacket c, tr, cr, br OPG/ST/MW, **tl** OPG/IB/AA, **bl** C; **front jacket flap** C; **back jacket** S; **back jacket flap** OPG/ST/MW; **2 tl** OPG/ST/MW, **tcl** OPG/ST/MW, **tcr** OPG/ST/MW, **tr** OPG/ST/MW, **cl** OPG/ST/MW, **cr** OPG/ST/MW, **bl** OPG/ST/MW, **bcl** OPG/ST/MW, **bcr** OPG/ST/MW; **3 tl** OPG/ST/MW, **tr** OPG/AJ, **c** OPG/ST/MW, **bl** OPG/ST/MW, **br** OPG/ST/MW; **8 tl** SL, **tr** V&A, **bl** M, **br** OPG/IB/MW; **9 tl** SL, **tr** PC, **bl** OPG/ST/MW, **br** C; **10** OPG/ST/MW; **11** OPG/ST/MW; **12** OPG/ST/MW; **13 t** OPG/ST/MW, **b** S; **14** OPG/ST/MW; **15** C; **16** OPG/ST; **17** OPG/AJ/RN; **18** OPG/ST/MW; **19** OPG/ST/MW; **20** OPG/ST/MW; **21** OPG/ST/MW; **22** MJW; **23** OPG/JH; **24** OPG/JM; **25** OPG/ST/MW; **26** OPG/AJ; **27** SL; **28** OPG/JM; **29** OPG/JM; **30** CNY; **31** CL; **32** SL; **33** OPG/ST/MW; **34** C; **35** S; **36 t** OPG/TR/PA, **bl** CL; **37 tr** PC, **b** OPG/ST/MW; **38 tl** OPG/IB/MW, **c** C, **br** OPG/ST/MW; **39 tl** SL, **tc** OPG/ST/MW, **tr** SL, **cl** SL, **cr** CL, **c** OPG/ST/MW; **40 tl** SL, **tc** OPG/IB/MW, **cl** SL, **cr** SL, **c** OPG/IB/MW, **br** SL; **41 tl** OPG/IB/MW, **tc** OPG/AJ, **tr** OPG/IB/MW, **bl** OPG/IB/MW, **bc** OPG/AJ; **42 tl** CL, **cl** CL, **c** OPG/IB/MW, **cr** CL, **bc** OPG/IB/MW; **43 tl** OPG/SC/NH, **tc** OPG/AJ, **tr** S, **cr** S, **bl** OPG/SC/NH, **bc** OPG/AJ; **45** OPG/AP; **46** BH; **47 tl** BH, **br** BH; **48** OPG/ST/MW; **49** OPG/ST/MW; **50 t** S, **b** OPG/ST/MW; **51 t** OPG/ST/MW, **bl** OPG/ST/MW, **br** OPG/ST/MW; **52 tl** S, **tr** OPG/ST/MW, **b** OPG/ST/MW; **53 l** S, **t** OPG/ST/MW, **br** OPG/ST/MW; **54 l** OPG/ST/MW, **r** OPG/ST/MW; **55 r** S, **b** OPG/ST/MW; **56 tl** S, **tr** C, **b** C; **57 all** OPG/ST/MW; **58 tl** S, **tr** OPG/ST/MW, **b** OPG/ST/MW; **59 tl** OPG/ST/MW, **br** OPG/ST/MW; **60 tl** OPG/ST/MW, **tr** OPG/ST/MW, **b** S; **61 tl** C, **c** OPG/ST/MW, **b** OPG/ST/MW; **62 l** OPG/ST/MW, **r** OPG/ST/MW; **63 t** OPG/ST/MW, **cl** OPG/ST/MW, **cr** OPG/ST/MW, **b** OPG/ST/MW; **64 tl** OPG/IB/MW, **tr** OPG/IB/MW, **b** MJW; **65 t** OPG, **tl** OPG/ST/MW, **tr** OPG/ST/MW, **b** OPG/ST/MW; **66 tl** OPG/ST/MW, **tr** OPG/ST/MW, **b** OPG/ST/MW; **67 tl** OPG/ST/MW, **tr** OPG/ST/MW, **b** S; **68 tl** S, **tr** S, **b** S; **69 tr** S, **c** S, **bl** S; **70 tl** OPG/ST/MW, **tr** OPG/ST/MW, **b** OPG/ST/MW; **71 tl** OPG/ST/MW, **tr** OPG/ST/MW, **b** OPG/ST/MW; **72 tr** S, **bl** S; **73 tr** S, **c** OPG/ST/MW, **b** OPG/ST/MW; **74 tl** C, **tr** C, **b** S; **75 l** OPG/ST/MW, **t** S, **br** C; **76 tr** S, **bl** S, **br** S; **77 tl** S, **cr** OPG/ST/MW, **b** OPG/ST/MW; **78 l** S, **r** OPG/ST/MW, **c** C; **79 tl** OPG/ST/MW, **tcr** OPG/ST/MW; **b** OPG/ST/MW; **80 tl** OPG/ST/MW, **tr** OPG/ST/MW, **b** OPG/ST/MW; **81 l** OPG/ST/MW, **r** OPG/ST/MW, **c** OPG/ST/MW; **82 tr** S, **bl** S, **tl** S; **83 bl** S, **br** S; **84 tl** OPG/ST/MW, **bl** OPG/ST/MW; **85 l** OPG/ST/MW, **tr** OPG/ST/MW, **br** OPG/ST/MW; **86 r** OPG/ST/MW, **bl** PC; **87 t** GVA, **c** GVA, **b** GVA; **88 r** S, **tl** S, **c** S; **89 t** S, **bl** S, **br** C; **90 t** OPG/ST/MW, **b** OPG/ST/MW; **91 t** OPG/AP, **cl** OPG/ST/MW, **cr** OPG/ST/MW, **bl** OPG/ST/MW, **br** OPG/ST/MW; **92 l** OPG/IB/MW, **bl** OPG/ST/MW, **br** OPG/ST/MW; **93 tl** OPG/IB/MW, **tc** SL, **bl** OPG/ST/MW, **br** OPG/ST/MW; **94 tl** OPG/ST/MW, **tr** OPG/ST/MW, **b** OPG/ST/MW; **95 tl** OPG/ST/MW, **tr** OPG/ST/MW, **b** OPG/ST/MW; **96 l** OPG/ST/MW, **r** OPG/ST/MW, **tc** S; **97 r** OPG/ST/MW, **t** OPG/ST/MW, **b** OPG/ST/MW; **98 tl** OPG/ST/MW, **tr** OPG/ST/MW, **b** OPG/ST/MW; **99 r** OPG/IB/MW, **tl** OPG/ST/MW, **bl** S; **100 t** OPG/ST/MW, **bl** OPG/ST/MW, **br** OPG/ST/MW; **101 tl** OPG/ST/MW, **tr** OPG/ST/MW, **b** OPG/ST/MW; **102 tl** GVA, **br** GVA; **103 tr** SK, **cl** OPG/ST/D&PA, **b** SK; **104 t** OPG/ST/MW, **b** OPG/ST/MW; **105 t** OPG/ST/MW, **bl** OPG/ST/MW, **b** C OPG/ST/MW, **br** OPG/ST/MW; **106 tl** OPG/ST/MW, **tr** OPG/ST/MW, **b** OPG/ST/MW; **107 t** OPG/ST/MW, **bl** OPG/ST/MW, **br** OPG/ST/MW; **108 l** OPG/ST/MW, **r** OPG/ST/MW; **109 t** OPG/ST/MW, **bl** OPG/ST/MW, **br** OPG/ST/MW; **110 tl** S, **tr** OPG/ST/MW, **bl** S, **br** OPG/ST/MW; **111 t** OPG/ST/MW, **c** OPG/ST/MW, **b** OPG/AJ/RN; **112** S; **113 tr** C, **cl** OPG/ST/MW, **cr** OPG/ST/MW, **bl** OPG/ST/MW, **br** OPG/ST/MW; **114 tl** S, **b** S; **115 t** OPG/ST/MW, **bl** OPG/ST/MW, **br** OPG/ST/MW; **116 t** GVA, **bl** FHB, **br** FHB; **117 r** SK, **t** PC, **b** SK; **118** C; **119 tl** S, **tr** OPG/ST/MW, **bl** OPG/ST/MW, **br** OPG/IB/MW; **120 t** OPG/ST/MW, **c** OPG/ST/MW, **b** OPG/ST/MW; **121 t** OPG/ST/MW, **b** OPG/ST/MW; **122** OPG/ST/MW; **123 t** OPG/ST/MW, **cl** OPG/ST/MW, **cr** OPG/ST/MW, **b** OPG/ST/MW; **124 l** OPG/ST/MW, **t** C; **125 t** OPG/ST/MW, **c** OPG/ST/MW, **b** OPG/ST/MW; **126 tl** S, **br** C; **127 t** C, **c** OPG/IB/MW, **b** GVA; **128 t** C, **b** C; **129 tl** C, **tr** C, **br** OPG/ST/MW, **br** OPG/ST/MW; **130 tl** FHB, **c** OPG/AJ/RN, **bl** GVA; **131 tl** GVA, **tr** GVA, **b** OPG/AJ/BH; **132 t** C, **b** OPG/ST/MW; **133 t** OPG/ST/MW, **bl** OPG/ST/MW, **br** OPG/ST/MW; **134 t** GVA, **bl** GVA, **br** GVA; **135 r** LN, **tl** LN, **b** OPG/IB/MW; **136 t** S, **bl** OPG/IB/MW, **br** OPG/ST/MW; **137 l** FHB, **tr** M, **b** C; **138 tl** OPG/ST/MW, **tr** CL, **b** S; **139 t** OPG/ST/MW, **c** OPG/IB/MW, **b** LN; **140 t** OPG/ST/MW, **b** OPG/ST/MW; **141 t** SL, bl OPG/ST/MW, **br** OPG/AJ/BH; **142 r** OPG/ST/MW, **tl** OPG/ST/MW, **bl** OPG/ST/MW; **143 t** OPG/ST/MW, **cl** OPG/ST/MW, **cr** OPG/ST/MW, **b** OPG/ST/MW; **144 l** S, **r** SL, **b** C; **145 t** OPG/ST/MW, **c** OPG/ST/MW, **bl** SAA, **br** SAA; **146 t** C, **b** C; **147 tl** C, **tr** C, **c** C, **b** C; **148 l** C, **r** C; **149 tl** C, **tr** C, **bl** S, **br** C; **150** OPG/ST/MW; **151 t** OPG/ST/MW, **bl** OPG/ST/MW, **bc** OPG/ST/MW, **bcr** OPG/ST/MW; **152 t** OPG/ST/MW, **b** OPG/ST/MW, **br** OPG/ST/MW; **153 tl** OPG/ST/MW, **tr** OPG/ST/MW, **b** OPG/ST/MW; **154 tl** M, **b** S; **155 tl** SL, **tr** M, **c** OPG/ST/MW, **b** OPG/IB/MW; **156 tl** OPG/ST/MW, **tr** OPG/ST/MW, **b** OPG/ST/MW; **157 r** OPG/ST/MW, **t** OPG/ST/MW, **b** OPG/ST/MW; **158 l** C, **r** S; **159 l** OPG/ST/MW, **tr** OPG/ST/MW, **b** SL; **160 tr** OPG/ST/MW, **b** OPG/ST/MW; **161 r** OPG/ST/MW, **t** OPG/ST/MW, **bl** OPG/IB/MW; **162** OPG/JM; **163** OPG/AJ

KEY
b bottom, **c** centre, **l** left, **r** right, **t** top
AA Alfie's Antique Market, 13-25 Church Street, London NW8 8DT; **AJ** A.J. Photographics; **AP** Amanda Patton; **BH** Broadfield House Glass Museum, Kingswinford, West Midlands DY6 9NS; **C** Christie's Images; **CL** Christie's, 8 King Street, St James's, London SW1; **D&PA** D. & P. Atkinson; **FHB** Frank H. Boos Gallery, Auctioneers and Appraisers, Bloomfield Hills, MI; **GVA** Green Valley Auctions Inc., Mt Crawford, VA; **IB** Ian Booth; **JH** Jacqui Hurst; **JM** James Merrell; **LN** Lillian Nassau Ltd, New York City, NY; **M** Mallett & Son (Antiques) Ltd, 141 New Bond Street, London W1Y 0BS; **MJW** Mark J. West, 39b High Street, Wimbledon, London SW19; **MW** Mark J. West; **NH** Nicholas Harris; **OPG** Octopus Publishing Group Ltd; **PA** Pars Antiques; **PC** Private Collection; **RN** Raymond Notley; **S** Sotheby's Picture Library, London; **SAA** Skinner, Auctioneers and Appraisers of Antiques and Fine Art, Boston, MA; **SC** Stuart Chorley; **SL** Sotheby's, 34-35 New Bond Street, London W1A; **ST** Steve Tanner, 2 Bleeding Heart Yard, London EC1N; **TR** Tim Ridley; **V&A** Victoria & Albert Museum, Cromwell Road, London SW7